The Manx Loghtan Story

The Decline and Revival of a Primitive Breed

By Peter Wade-Martins

Published by
Geerings of Ashford
in association with
The Rare Breeds Survival Trust

1990

Published by Geerings of Ashford Ltd.,
Cobbs Wood House,
Ashford,
Kent,
TN23 1EP.

Typeset by Spire Origination,
Kerrison Road,
Norwich,
Norfolk,
NR1 1JA.

Design and maps by Geerings of Ashford Ltd.
Illustrations by Sue White.

British Library Cataloguing in Publication Data
Wade-Martins, Peter
  The Manx Loghtan story.
  1. Livestock. Loghtan Manx, Sheep
  I. Title
  636.32

  ISBN 0-9513042-7-5

Geerings wish to acknowledge with gratitude the support received from the
Rare Breeds Survival Trust and its chief executive, Alastair Dymond for the
publication of this book.

Contents

List of black and white plates

List of Colour Plates

List of Figures

List of Tables

Note on the spelling of 'Loghtan'

Readers will notice that the spelling of the Manx word for the colour of the wool varies throughout the book. This is because there has been no 'right' way to spell the word over the centuries; 'Manx' and 'Manks' is another example. In quotations the spelling used in the original has been copied faithfully each time. The island breed society is most particular about using 'Loaghtan', while the author has followed the shorter 'Loghtan' spelling preferred by the Rare Breeds Survival Trust.

Acknowledgements

Two institutions have played a leading role in the preservation of the breed, and they have both been especially helpful during the preparation of this book. At the Manx Museum in Douglas, Isle of Man, Ann Harrison and her staff in the museum library have done everything possible to assist with documentary research, and Larch Garrad has patiently answered the author's many questions about the management of the museum flock. At the Rare Breeds Survival Trust, based at the National Agricultural Centre at Stoneleigh near Coventry, their Chief Executive, Alastair Dymond, has been most encouraging during the preparation of the book; both he and the Trust's Technical Consultant, Lawrence Alderson, have provided much advice and guidance.

In the Isle of Man, Jack Quine stands out as the one man alive today whose personal commitment has saved the breed; he has also given unfailing support by digging deep into his memory and by making his own papers freely available for research. Mary Aldrich, Alec and Alex Maddrell, Barbara Platt, Kenneth Whitehead, Malcolm Wright, Bob Penrice, William Bealby-Wright, Joe Henson and Ken Briggs have likewise searched their memories and given generously of their time and advice. Harvey Briggs compiled extracts of entries for Loghtan classes from catalogues of the Isle of Man agricultural shows and provided other most useful information. Lawrence Alderson calculated the amount of influence Shetland sheep had on Caesar Bacon's Loghtan flock and made a number of helpful comments on drafts of the book. Dr. Kim Bryan kindly organised the photography of the specimens in the Natural History Museum, and Mr. V.J.A. Manton provided copies of records of the Loghtans kept at Whipsnade Zoo.

Fenella Bazin, Marjorie Crowe, John Bregazzi and their colleagues in the Manx Loaghtan Sheep Breed Society most warmly welcomed British members of the Rare Breeds Survival Trust to the island in May 1988 and did much to establish excellent relations between the British and Manx sheep breeders.

Many people and organisations have kindly provided photographs; these are all gratefully acknowledged in the plate captions. The Isle of Man Philatelic Bureau provided the 5p and 20p stamps, while the Pobjoy Mint provided the 1p coin. Similarly, the Isle of Man Government Treasury supplied the 5p and 10p coins to be photographed.

Finally, special thanks must go to those early breeders in Britain who responded to my circulars and letters by providing information and also to the various people who have kindly agreed to their copyright material being quoted or reproduced in the book.

Castlemilk Moorit sheep:
The story of the origins of these sheep could not have been pieced together without the help of Sir Rupert Buchanan-Jardine, whose kindness is gratefully acknowledged.

Forword

The British Isles have a remarkable inheritance of domestic livestock, with over 50 native breeds of sheep ranging from the primitive prehistoric Soay through to the eighteenth and nineteenth century creations like to Suffolk. Some of these breeds will be fashionable when they suit the farming practices of the day, while others rapidly decline into extinction.

However, fashions do change as farming methods evolve, so that characteristics of a breed which are not required under one system may be ideally suited to the next. That is why the Rare Breeds Survival Trust has such an important role to play in British agriculture. It has established beyond doubt the importance of preserving minority breeds. Twenty three British breeds of pigs, sheep cattle and horses became extinct during this century up until 1974; since then none have been lost, thanks largely to the work of the Trust.

Past generations were less aware of the advantages of genetic conservation, yet there are heroic stories of breeds being maintained against all the odds. The Manx Loghtan Story is one of these; it is a fascinating account of how the breed was nurtured by a series of dedicated people determined that this important part of Manx farming history should not die. While the story is ostensibly about sheep, it is really one of human endeavour.

An important part of the Trust's work is to increase interest in rare breeds amongst farmers and non-farmers alike, and this book will contribute greatly to that work. The Trust is to be congratulated on encouraging the author to assemble this account of how a breed was saved before memories fade any further. While this is the first breed history to be published with the support of the Trust, let us hope that it will be followed by many more.

The Duchess of Devonshire
President of The Rare Breeds Survival Trust, 1988-9

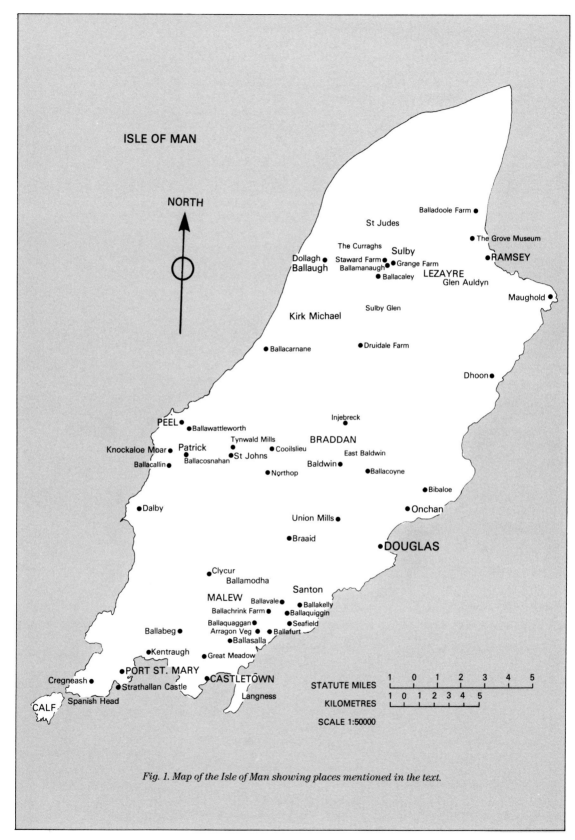

Fig. 1. Map of the Isle of Man showing places mentioned in the text.

Introduction

The Manx Loghtan is still one of the rarest breeds of sheep in the British Isles, with about 700 breeding ewes in Britain and a further 600 in the Isle of Man. A small sheep, with mature ewes weighing about 40kg., it has two, four or even six horns and a ginger-brown or 'moorit' fleece. The breed originated in the Isle of Man where the word 'Loghtan' is a rather imprecise colour term describing 'drab, dun, dusky or greyish-brown'. It may be derived from the two Manx words *Lugh* (mouse) and *Dhoan* (brown) or from *Lhosht dhoan* (burnt brown). Not only is the meaning a little imprecise in the Manx language, but so also is the spelling, for it can have at least as many forms as the sheep can have horns. The variety of spellings can be seen in the many quotations in the book where the original version has been faithfully copied each time. The form used in the title of the book is the simplest and the one adopted by the Rare Breeds Survival Trust. The breed society on the island, however, spells it as 'Loaghtan'.

The breed is descended from a primitive type of sheep common in the later prehistoric period over much of Britain. In modern times it has survived only in the remoter parts of the British Isles, where the Hebridean, Boreray, Shetland and North Ronaldsay breeds are all close relatives of the Manx.

This small fine-boned and very agile sheep has come close to extinction three times in the last 100 years, but until the eighteenth century it must have covered the Manx hills in thousands. Then, the breed had several colours: white, black, grey as well as the famous Loghtan which was then rather unusual. The story of how the breed survived over the last century is a fascinating one, told in full here for the first time. Much previously unpublished information has come to light while this book was being prepared. Some of the story has been written down from the memories of people who witnessed the events. Gaps remain, even for the post-war period, and the writer would be delighted to hear of anyone who can provide further details of this enthralling story.

Since 1973 the Rare Breeds Survival Trust has done much to popularise the little-known breeds, and it has been able to demonstrate the importance of conserving types which may be currently out of fashion but which have a role to play in the modern farming industry. While primitive breeds have their disadvantages, in particular the slow speed at which lambs reach maturity, they also have some remarkable assets. They have an amazing ability to thrive on a relatively low level of nutrition, and they seldom suffer the afflictions of more improved breeds. They usually lamb without much help, and the ewes have very strong mothering instincts. When put to a modern Down ram the result is a very respectable cross-bred lamb. It will develop into just what today's meat industry requires, all for relatively little input.

The Manx Loghtan is an attractive sheep which looks well in parkland and in orchard, and the coloured fleece is sought after by spinners. An easy-to-look-after animal, it is ideal for the beginner and it has potential yet to be exploited by the commercial sheep industry.

This book explains how the breed was saved from extinction several times and then reached the numbers we have today. The present state of the breed is discussed and ideas for the future are explored. But for the dedication and foresight of just a few, we would not have today a breed which has enriched the lives of many people all over Britain interested in small-scale sheep farming.

In the Beginning
(up to 1895)

The Manx mountain sheep

The Manx Loghtan is all that survives of a breed of Manx hill sheep which was common on the upland farms in the Isle of Man until the eighteenth century. Gradually, it was replaced by improved British and other imported breeds. This 'Manx mountain sheep', as it was called, was a primitive short-tailed horned sheep similar to other early breeds in the north and west of Scotland, the Shetlands, the Faroes and Iceland. All these sheep had a variety of colours, as seen in the Shetland and North Ronaldsay breeds today.

Of this ancient stock, which has its origins in prehistory, we have left today in the British Isles the Boreray, the Hebridean, the North Ronaldsay and the Shetland as well as the Manx Loghtan. Their variety is due partly to the isolation of one group from another and partly to man's selection for particular characteristics to suit local needs and circumstances. The Manx was especially good at surviving on poor grazing in high upland where more modern breeds would perish, whilst the North Ronaldsay had adapted to live on seaweed. All are two-horned, but the Manx, Hebridean and Iceland sheep have the multi-horned trait as well. The Shetland was multi-horned up until the 1920s, whilst similar breeds in the Hebrides and on the main island of St. Kilda, were all extinct by 1900. This group had a wide range of colours: white, black, grey, brown and piebald, and they represent the descendants of sheep common from the Iron Age to the eighteenth century. The Jacob, whose long tail demonstrates that it has been crossed with other breeds, may owe its horn pattern to the same short- tailed group. Alternatively, it may have a Spanish or Mediterranean origin.

More primitive still, representing a survival from the Bronze Age, are the small brown Soays which remained unchanged because of their isolation out in the Atlantic on the St. Kilda group of islands.

Archaeological evidence

The origins of the Manx mountain sheep are not yet fully understood, and progress in the field will depend on the results of archaeological research, both on the Isle of Man and elsewhere.

The bones of the modern Manx Loghtan are said to have two characteristic features which distinguish them from more improved breeds. One is that the horn cores are D-shaped in section, like that of a goat; the other is the position in the femur of an opening for a blood vessel which is lower down the bone shaft than in modern breeds. Following the programme of archaeological excavations at Peel Castle which cut through deep deposits going right back to prehistoric times, there are now bone groups available for study from Iron Age, early Christian, medieval and later periods. It will be possible to study these bones to see how domesticated animals have evolved on the island over the centuries, but so far the results of this painstaking work are not available.

The earliest descriptions

There are only a few early descriptions of the breed, and references to Loghtan garments are scarce. William Blundell's manuscript history of the Isle of Man of about 1650 mentions the Loghtans, and it is clear from his description of Manx sheep that the Loghtan colour was unusual and the wool was highly prized.

> The wool of their sheep is very good, but not to be compared to our Cotswold or Leicester, yet have they a little and but a little of a certain wool which I attempt one of the rerities of the island, and far exceeds their other wool in fineness. This sort of wool they call Laughton wool, and the sheep which beareth that coloured wool, the Manksmen call the grayish coloured Laughton in the language, howbeit this coloured wool to me seemed rather to resemble the dear colour, inclining to fevill mort, and near but no so high tincted as the hair colour. Mr. Chaloner calleth it a sand colour and not unfitly; but the rarity of this wool is very remarkable, for it is no certain place to be found in all the island. It is a monady, for one only sheep of the whole flock will have this coloured wool in any part of the Island, and they are observed not to impart that colour to their lambs. Wherefore there is not much of it to be had thro'out the whole Island. Yet I did see the late Lord of Man, James Earl of Darby, to wear an entire suit of that wool.

The tenth Earl of Derby in the early eighteenth century also wore cloth of this wool.

A previously unknown early mention of a Loghtan item has recently been discovered in the will of Margrett Crobin who died in 1697: the entry reads as follows:

> ..... Item she bequeathed to Edmon Postley as much kearley as would make him a cote Item she bequeathed to her sister in law Joney Waterson a laughten waistcott and petticott Item bequeathed to Margaret Corrin a yard of linin cloth; Item bequeathed to Henry Corrin an ew, and she left that her made linine should be kept for her daughters use: Item: she nominated and appointed her daughter Joney Crebin her sold executrix of all the rest of her goods movable and unmovable whatsoever, ...

'Kearley' or 'kheeir' was an abbreviation for 'kheein-leear', the more common unimproved brown/grey wool (p.5). A garment made of Loghtan must have been sufficiently special to deserve a mention in this way. All her wool was valued at 3s 6d and the sheep at 6s.

The eighteenth century

The fact that Loghtan wool was rather unusual is also clear from Sacheverell's account in his *Short History of the Isle of Man* published in 1702:

> They have also a reasonable quantity of sheep, and some improve in their breed very much, but of these they have barely enough to answer the necessities of the country. They have a remarkable sort they call Laughtown-sheep; and the wool Laughtown-wool, which when carefully dressed makes a cloth near to hair colour, which is one of the greatest rarities of the country, especially since the lambs seldom follow the colour of the sheep, though I suppose it is because they are not kept unmixed, which I have found true to experience.

Gibson's 1772 edition of Camden's *Britiannia* mentions the sheep, but only briefly:

> Amongst the sheep they have some called loughtan of a buff colour; the wool is fine, and makes a pretty cloth without any dye.

Hand-woven garments, for which the colours of the loghtan fleeces were ideally suited, gradually gave way to mechanised production, as Larch Garrad explains, in her most useful summary of the breed, published in *100 Years of Heritage* (1986):

> From about the middle of the eighteenth century larger scale water-powered spinning and weaving and commercial dyeing grew in importance in the Isle of Man. This meant that coloured sheep lost their popularity. The natural darker wools had been valued to provide yarn from which to knit stockings and for the weaving of practical outerwear, particularly for the men. Used in weaving checks and plaids it could be over-dyed in the piece to give a subtle range of hues. With a commercial woollen industry this changed. The manufacturers disliked dark wools as they created problems in cleaning the machines after they had been processed and all the cards had to be replaced, as trapped dark fibres would contaminate the wool. William Kelly, proprietor of the Union Mills, 'at the sign of the flail and the fleece', as his card-money stated, did much to accelerate the decline of the native dark-wooled strains by paying a premium for white fleeces. The white ones could be graded up towards a longer-stapled wool sheep, rather than a general purpose animal. The dark ones seemed doomed.

The eighteenth century was the great period of agricultural improvement, as new methods of crop rotation, developed first in Norfolk in the 1660s, eventually reached the remoter areas. David Robertson in his *Tour through the Isle of Man* described in 1794 how Manx agriculture was waking up to new ideas being brought in by farmers from outside:

> Of late years several English farmers, sinking under the accumulated taxes of their own country, have retired to a land, as yet exempt from such oppression. Here they enjoy peace and abundance; while the success attending their agricultural labours seems at length to have raised the Manks from their lethargy. The marshy grounds are now drained; the waste lands enclosed, and nourished with lime, marle and sea-weed; cultivation begins to throw a rich verdure over hill and vale....Beef seldom exceeds 2d. a pound; mutton is equally cheap, and perhaps the most delicious in the world.

In the woollen mills the coloured wools were described as 'Kheeir', the standard mix of grey, black and Loghtan wools usual in nineteenth-century tweed. This is presumably the same word which Blundell was referring to in 1650: 'that coloured wool, the Manksmen call the greyish coloured Loghtan in their language' (p.4).

John Feltham in 1798 said that the natives liked cloth and stockings made of the loghtan wool, but there is no detailed description of the breed or how it was managed until the nineteenth century. By then the substitution of Manx mountain sheep for imported breeds was well under way.

The nineteenth century
In 1811, George Woods described the variety of sheep then on the Isle of Man:

> Sheep are fed chiefly on the up-lands. The ancient stock is very small and hardy, much like the south-down of England, and endures the severest weather. When fat, their usual weight is from five to eight pounds per quarter. Their meat is excellent. This is still the breed upon the uplands and mountains; but in the lowlands a larger sort has been introduced. Two pounds and a half is the average weight of the fleeces of the small sheep, and six or seven pounds of the large ones. It is not of the finest or longest staple. The sheep are not washed previously to their being sheared. Besides the two sorts already mentioned, there is a peculiar breed called Laughton, having wool of a light brown or snuff colour, These are not accounted hardy, and are more difficult to fatten than the other sorts. The cloth made of their wool is much liked by the natives, and on this account only is the breed preserved.

Woods seems to be saying that the white mountain sheep were different from the Loghtans, but this was probably because he didn't realise that the

Loghtan was just a colour variant of the hill breed he first described.

In contrast, we have in Thomas Quayle's 1812 *General View of Agriculture of the Isle of Man* a much more informed and detailed account. In this remarkably important piece, Quayle describes the old breed, with its variety of colours; he then describes the new breeds which were gradually taking over. Finally, he discusses the problems which these new breeds were bringing with them. Sheep scab was rife; 'at present its virulence is remarkable'. Maggots had become a common occurrence, while the mountain sheep were renowned for not being susceptible to them. Foot rot was also a problem they were learning to cope with.

The Isle of Man has also an indigenous breed of sheep, little and hardy, but of mean appearance. with high backs and narrow ribs, slow feeders, and long in coming to maturity. The ewes are sometimes polled, sometimes horned; the rams always horned. Their general colour is white; but many are grey, some black, and a few of a peculiar colour, approaching to that of an unblanched bitter almond. which in the language of the country is termed *laughton*. In the whole breed, a general distinctive mark is said to appear in a laughton-coloured patch in the back of the neck, which in the sheep of other colours disappears as the wool grows. Parents of the ordinary colours occasionally produce laughton lambs; and vice versa. Another peculiarity attaches to the breed in the conformation of the tail, which has some resemblance to that of a goat, thick at the root, and tapering to the extremity. The lamb is a remarkably sinewy active animal; playful like a fawn, and graceful in his movements. This breed appears to have been once widely dispersed. A cargo of Iceland sheep, which a gentleman resident in the Isle of Man had an opportunity of examining, resembled the Manks precisely, and in every point; having amongst them a laughton individual. In St. Kilda there appear to be sheep of that colour.

In the Shetland Isles they appear of the same parentage; and they so nearly agree with No. 13, in Culley's List, called the *Dun-faced*, as to make it probable that each are derived from the same original. In quality of wool, and in flavour of mutton, they bear strong resemblance to the North Welsh; and in wool to the sheep of Delamere-forest. It is observed that sheep of the laughton colour are more tender and slower feeders than their brethren. But the esteem in which cloth and stockings manufactured of their wool are held by some Manksmen, as a sort of national distinction, leads to the preservation of sheep of this colour. From the influx of foreign breeds, it is however in some danger of being lost. One instance has occurred of the half-breed South-down and Manks retaining its laughton colour with the make of its English parentage. Several attempts have been made by the introduction of selected animals of the breeds from England, to improve the fleece, and hasten the maturity of the animal. None can be made for the improvement of the mutton; the flavour of which is admitted to be superior, when the animal has been kept to a proper age, to any of them. Pure Merino rams, those of its fourth cross with the Ryeland, the new Leicester, and Southdown, have been severally introduced. The cross of each of these with Manks ewes, promises well. The two latter have well formed heavy lambs; and in particular the cross between the South-down and Manks is little inferior, in any respect, the male parent.

The Ryeland Merino ram has been put to a lot of Manks ewes, selected by a manufacturer as bearing the finest wool, and their progeny dispersed throughout the island. The result of the experiment, still in progress, promises favourably. The wool, (in) 1811, of a flock of Manks-Merino sold, unwashed, as 4s. per lb.; the blue cloth to be manufactured from it being all bespoken at £1.10s. per yard. The half-breed Manks-Merino lambs do not, it must be admitted, promise to be good feeders.

The greater part of the native sheep are removed during the summer to the mountains. On the approach to winter, they return to the lower grounds, and are lanketed[1]; often meeting at home with more scanty fare than on the mountains.

When the ploughing commences, they are turned by the smaller farmers into the newly ploughed fields, and fare sumptuously on the weeds and their roots, which the sheep dig up with great assiduity. Thirty sheep have been observed to derive their whole sustenance from one single ploughed field for two months. The treatment of the improved breeds is more liberal; but the wretched state of the fences makes the lanket indispensable to all. Strange as it may seem, it is universally asserted that the Manx sheep will not eat either hay or turnips; but if such be their rule, it must be allowed that they are not often put in the way of temptation to violate it ......

Manx fleece is all carding wool. It contains black hairs; and wool of widely different degrees of fineness. The proportion of fine wool in each, varies from one-eight to one-fourth part. The sheep are not washed before clipping; and the wool delivered in a foul state loses from one-third to a full half in cleaning, the finer wool losing the greatest proportion. It is stated by the manufacturer, that Manks wool, compared with South-down wool of an equal degree of fineness: is softer to the touch, works more smoothly, mills finer, and stretches better. In sheep of the same flock, a striking difference is observable; if part have been fed on good pasture, the remainder on indifferent, the wool of the former grows too deep for the purpose of manufacture, though not materially coarser. Much mischief has been and still is done to the quality of Manks wool by the importation, many years ago, of a Scotch breed called the *Linton*[2], the wool of which is coarse, and neither fit for combing nor carding. Rams of this breed are still indiscriminately placed on the mountains.

Good and ill are ever found intimately mixed; with the improvement of carcass and wool, the imported breeds have introduced diseases hitherto unknown in a Manks flock. The scab in particular has made great progress. As usually happens, when any malady for the first time attacks any race of animals, men or brutes, whose progenitors and themselves have been wholly unaccustomed to it, at present its virulence is remarkable, and no adequate remedy has hitherto been generally applied. Against the maggots, a solution of allum, poured at an early period into the wounds which they occasion, has been found effectual. The sheep attacked with foot-rot are walked across hot lime; but sufficient care to keep the foot clean has not been afterwards taken......

Parliament has permitted the annual exportation of 300 sheep from certain ports in Great Britain to the Isle of Man.

A number of significant points emerge from this description. The breed was already on the decline. It was being replaced by, and crossed with, the Linton or Scottish Blackface and probably also the Cheviot on the hills and by Southdowns, Ryelands, Leicesters, and Merino sheep on the lowlands. With imports being introduced into the island at the rate of at least 300 a year, many of them rams, it was not going to be long before the indigenous population would be overwhelmed. Once again we are told that the mountain breed was generally white, but many were grey, some were black and *a few* were loghtan. The loghtan colour was regarded as rather special; cloth and knitted garments made from this wool were highly prized. It seems that sheep of this colour were being singled out for breeding because of their popularity. As moorit is recessive to all other colours it breeds true; thus, it was relatively easy to fix it as a characteristic of the breed.

The Manx mountain sheep were highly regarded for their ability to survive on the meanest of diets, living in ploughed fields in winter eating weeds and their roots. It was thought that they did not like hay or turnips, but were seldom given the chance to demonstrate this, as the better winter feed was always kept back for the improved breeds!

The downward slide seemed irreversible
In early February 1862 there is a charming report in the newspaper *Mona's Herald* of early lambing results in a flock kept by an enthusiast called John Corlett at Ballaugh.

EXTRAORDINARY FECUNDITY. — We stated last week that ten lambs of the pure Manx mountain breed had been yeaned (born) this season by ewes belonging to the flock of Mr. John Corlett, on the estate of Dollaugh Beg, in the Parish of Ballaugh. We have now to add that since our last publication eleven more have been yeaned from the same flock, making in all 21 lambs. Surely the whole island may safely be challenged to produce such a number at so early a period in the year.[3]

In 1867 in an address to the Isle of Man Farmer's Club, a speaker, whose name is not recorded, said 'The Manx native sheep .... just now appears to be giving way to some other breed, hereafter to occupy the mountain pastures'. Despite the breed's obvious advantages, the downward slide of the mountain sheep seemed irreversible, that is until Bacon plucked the breed back from the brink of extinction in 1895.

Footnotes
(1) Lankets were ropes used to tie a front leg to an opposite rear leg of troublesome sheep to stop them wandering away prior to the erection of wire fences. Latterly, these ropes were made from cocoanut hair.

(2) The Linton was the main ancestor of the Scottish Blackface and the Swaledale.

(3) A Corlett of Ballaugh was later given a ewe by Caesar Bacon sometime after 1896, but there is no reason to assume continuity of the same flock over 35 years.

Caesar Bacon
(1895-1916)

The Bacon family

The Bacon family arrived in the Isle of Man in 1724. Joseph Bacon (1694-1728) came from Staward in Northumberland, and settled near Sulby, in Lezayre, at a farm called Ballabrooie which he renamed 'Staward Farm'[1]. The second marriage of his son, John (1728-1809), brought the Santon property of Ballakilley at the south end into the family estates, and they renamed this farm 'Seafield'. John's mother-in-law was called Margaret Caesar, and the next three generations of Bacon all kept the name Caesar. They resided at Seafield, but retained the larger Staward estate. The Seafield and Staward farms were to play leading roles in the unfolding story of how the Loghtans were saved from extinction.

The third Bacon was Major Caesar Bacon (1791-1876) of the 23rd Light Dragoons who fought at Waterloo, although his regiment only managed to join the battle late in the day. He also fought at Quartre Bras and was twice wounded before retiring from the army in 1818.

The family had a tradition of being innovative agriculturalists, and Staward was rebuilt as a model farm in the 1840s. A stonemason is said to have been brought over from Northumberland to work at Staward, and there is a date stone of 1842 over the front arch together with a boar, the family emblem (*Plate C3*). The buildings were laid out around a courtyard with stables, cart sheds, loose boxes, a beef house, turnip and straw houses and stalls for milking cows. In one corner is a mill house which had a water wheel to power a Clayton and Shuttleworth thrashing machine, installed in 1843. This used water supplied from a long aqueduct, partly supported on stone pillars, taking water from higher up the Sulby River. These buildings were the work of Major Caesar Bacon who farmed on the island after he left the army in 1818 until his death in 1876.

The last in the line was John Caesar Bacon (1870-1916), the grandson of the war hero, and it was he who saved the Manx mountain sheep from extinction at the end of the nineteenth century. When he inherited the estates from his father, Captain John Joseph Bacon (1837-1909) he came into considerable wealth; his house at Seafield was described as 'quite an Elysium, commanding every comfort with exceptional scenery' (*Plates 1 and C1-2*).

Robert Quirk

Bacon took an interest in the survival of the sheep and gathered together at Staward and Seafield most of the animals remaining on the island at that time. There is an account of how this happened by a friend of his, Edward Christian, written down much later in October 1938 by P.W. Caine for the *Isle of Man Weekly Times*:

> Mr. Bacon's original flock, Mr. Christian understood, came from Colonel Anderson's, and Colonel Anderson's from the flock of Mr. Quirk, of the Abbey Lands, Onchan — not Baldwin, though East Baldwin is near by.

> Until these sales to Colonel Anderson and others — including the late Joseph Clarke, saddler, of Douglas — Quirk's was the only loaghtan flock in the Island.

Every other farmer had given them up. Quirk was a very curious character. He used to plough with a horse and a heifer, and the seed box of his turnip drill was an old top hat!

1. Caesar Bacon standing on the lawn at Seafield, date unknown. (Photo courtesy of William Bealby-Wright)

A version of this story was actually published in Bacon's lifetime in A.L.J. Gosset's most useful book *Shepherds of Britain* (1911):

> The race had become almost extinct in the Isle of Man in the earlier part of the last century, their place being taken by larger sheep brought over by Scotsmen who rented Manx commons. A Manxman in Baldwin, Quirk by name, who was of a conservative disposition, kept some of the old stock. He was quite a character, and believed, as he put it, 'the oul' times were bes' for all.' He ploughed with oxen, and would not have any new-fangled English improvements about his farm, but held on with his poor little loaghtans while his neighbours went in for the larger English and Scots breeds which paid them better. Thus loaghtans were being gradually displaced for such breeds as the Shropshire and Leicester in the low-lands, and by the Scotch mountain breed in the highlands. Many years after, Colonel Anderson, who still lives in the island, on passing through Baldwin, high up in the fastness of the Manx mountains, there saw these sheep. He brought some to his place in Michael, and later on other landowners also bought some of them. In these days when picturesque, even if less useful, types are gradually passing away, it is refreshing to hear of conservative Quirk and those who fol-lowed his example.

So, the first recorded man to whom we are indebted for the survival of the breed was the 'conservative Quirk', an eccentric farmer at Ballacoyn who had held on to old ways and old livestock when everyone around him was busily improving and modernising Manx farming. This was the first of a number of occasions when the right person happened to be involved at the right time to conserve the breed. Quirk sounds a most colourful character, and it is pity we know so little about him.

Bacon's breeding programme

One flock book of Bacon's survives, covering the period 1895-1909, and there, on the opening page, is the name of the first ram he used, 'Manaman beg', bred by Robert Quirk. The four foundation ewes were elderly sheep from Captain Windus, bred about 1887 'from the stock of Robert Quirk'. Other breeders from whom he obtained rams over the years were Thomas Bridson (in 1896), J. Quaye or Quayle (in 1899); Harold Macbeth of Arragon Veg in Santon (in

1899), J.Q. Cannell of Ballacarnane in Michael (in 1901) and Edward Christian of Ballacallin (in 1907).

There are also entries in the flock book for the introduction of four ewe lambs and three ewes from the Shetlands in 1897. The lambs had been first prize winners at the Shetland show at Lerwick in that year. Presumably, he had been on a trip to the Shetlands and had attended the Shetland show looking for suitable stock to strengthen his small, rather inbred, flock. He later built up his numbers by buying in 5 Manx ewes from Col. Anderson at Cooley Lodge, Michael, for mating in 1898 and a further four in 1900, as well as a few from other people. The only imported sheep shown in the flock book were the seven ewes from the Shetlands (*Plate 3*). The offspring from them were then used in the grading-up programme.

From the flock book it is possible to calculate the amount of influence the Shetlands subsequently had on Bacon's flock. A regular pattern seems to have been established during the years 1901 to 1907 inclusive; an analysis of all 86 lambs born during this period shows that 33.7% of the lambs carried Shetland blood, but the overall contribution of the Shetland introduction was only 6.0%[2]. Clearly, Bacon designed his crossing programme so that the Shetlands had a minimal long-term effect on his native stock.

By the numbers mated each year, one can see how he increased the size of the flock over 8 years from 1895 to 1903.

Numbers recorded in Bacon's flock book

Years	Ewes mated	Rams used
1895	4	1
1896	11	2
1897	17	1
1898	31	2
1899	35	3
1900	44	3
1901	36	4
1902	39	4
1903	46	4
1904	24	2
1905	32	3
1906	35	3
1907	39	3
1908	34	?

(Note: Whilst lambings are recorded, the entries are difficult to interpret, because they consist of a list of numbers, horizontal dashes, 'w' signs, crosses and circles (*Plate 3*). It is therefore not possible to calculate lambing numbers or percentages.)

The numbers rose from Robert Quirk's four ewes and ram in 1895 to a peak of 46 ewes mated to four rams in 1903. The drop from 46 to 24 in 1904 corresponded to a major sale held that October (p.13). Numbers built up afterwards, but by his death in 1916 they were down again to 24 (p.26). At the dispersal sales in 1916 the Manx mountain sheep were divided between Staward and Seafield Farms. Presumably, the flock had been regularly kept on both farms, although the locations of the stock are not shown in the flock book. Breeding details after 1909 are not recorded, because entries were transferred that year to another book which has not survived.

Bacon himself was a bachelor, and was certainly a popular and distinguished figure amongst Manx farmers[3]. He was a J.P., a churchwarden, a member of the Santon School Board, chairman of the parish commissioners,

2. Caesar Bacon (centre) as master of the Isle of Man Hunt, with his hounds at Seafield, date unknown. (Photo courtesy of William Bealby-Wright)

Captain of the Parish and Master of the Isle of Man Hunt (*Plates 2 and 6*). At parish elections he seems to have always topped the polls. We know he regularly used his Loghtan wool for his suits. 'Mr. Bacon's undyed light-brown clothes made him quite a picturesque figure.'

George Curphey, now 89 and living in an old people's home in Douglas, used to live in Santon, and his brother was a gardener at Seafield. He remembers Bacon as a tall figure who was often seen riding about the parish on horseback wearing a large black bowler hat. Bacon was renowned for keeping the gardens and the farm in 'apple-pie order'.

The only picture we have of him with his Loghtans is the one in Gosset's book (*Plate 5*). His hobby was pedigree livestock farming, and he specialised in breeding Shorthorn and Longhorn cattle (*Plate 4*), Shropshire and Manx mountain sheep, and various types of poultry. We know that he travelled around the Hebrides, the Faroes, the Shetlands and Iceland studying sheep, and he was renowned for the quality of his Longhorns and his Shropshires. In 1899 he exhibited a Shropshire shearling ram 'which was greatly admired and pronounced by competent gentlemen to be the best ram ever seen on the island'. He was constantly winning prizes for cattle and sheep at the Isle of Man agricultural shows. On the arable side, Bacon developed a new variety of potato.

Bacon was clearly a progressive farmer who did not wish to loose sight of old Manx breeds. If he was alive today he would probably make an ideal candidate for election to the Council of the Rare Breeds Survival Trust.

Bacon's annual sales

For 22 years, from 1894 to 1915, Bacon held each autumn a sale of his surplus stock. The sales were at Seafield on the flat field behind the farm buildings (*Plate C1*) until 1913, when they were moved to Dick's Mart at Ballasalla nearby. Mr. Thomson, his auctioneer, always ensured that the sale was well advertised beforehand, and then there was usually a sale report in the *Isle of Man Weekly Times* the following week. These advertisements and the sale reports provide a useful, if incomplete, record of the animals he sold and who bought them. As the years went by his sale became a popular event, which was no doubt helped by the fact that Bacon always 'gave the company present a good substantial luncheon'. All items were carefully catalogued, although no sale catalogues have survived. The first time mountain sheep appeared at his sales was in 1900 when he entered seven 'Manx and Shetland cross stock ewes': the only time Shetland cross sheep were mentioned in sale details; later, they were always described as 'pure'.

The notice in the *Isle of Man Weekly Times* of his major 1904 sale, when he reduced his mountain sheep flock to almost half, is worth quoting in full:

3. The pages in Bacon's flock book with the entry for the seven Shetland ewes imported in 1897. The upper half shows the parentage of the ewes in the flock. The lower half provides details of mating and lambing for each ewe for each year. Bacon usually gave his rams interesting names like Tharooushtey, Manaman beg 3rd, The Miller, Excelsior and Mickey The Twin. (Photo courtesy of the Manx Museum)

THE SEAFIELD ANNUAL SALE

On Thursday, October 13, Mr Thomson will hold an important sale at Seafield, Santon, of valuable pedigree and cross-bred cattle, Shire horses, Shropshire and Manx mountain sheep, large white Yorkshire pigs, Manx game and other poultry. Mr J.C.Bacon's reputation as a breeder of high-class stock is a sufficient guarantee of the sterling quality and value of the stock, amongst which will be found some very desirable lots of the best breeding and character, whilst comment on the flock of Shropshires is scarcely necessary, they being bred from the finest strain obtainable. Special attention is called to the Manx mountain sheep, whose many valuable qualities are not sufficiently well-known in and outside their own Island. This variety is undoubtedly the hardiest breed of sheep in the British Isles, wintering out on hills where other sheep would barely find subsistence during the summer months. They yield a carcass of excellent mutton of that game flavour so much liked by epicures; (they) also produce a fine texture of wool. One particular feature is their almost complete immunity from 'the fly', not a single specimen of the present flock, which has been in existence for 10 years, having ever been attacked by maggots. As a park sheep, also, they have a strong claim for favour. Their various colours , beautiful symmetry, and handsome four-horned heads usually carried by the rams, continue to give them a most ornamental appearance. Concluding, a careful perusal of the sale catalogue will well repay intending purchasers.

4. Caesar Bacon with one of his Shorthorn cows, 'Ruby Maid 2nd', date unknown. He was renowned for his breeding of Longhorn and Shorthorn cattle and Shropshire sheep. (Photo courtesy of William Bealby-Wright)

Although much of this is the auctioneer's attempt to promote the sale, it does seem to reflect the genuine respect in which Bacon's livestock was held by Manx farmers. There is also behind all this an obvious attempt by Bacon himself to promote the Manx mountain sheep breed.

At the 1904 sale the ewes averaged 21 shillings each, and the flock book shows that when he was selling mountain sheep privately he was charging about £1 each. At the sales he was receiving three times as much for his Shropshires, so there remained a significant price difference between the two breeds.

The following information on the numbers of mountain sheep sold at the annual sales and who bought them provides some insight into these events. Sadly, however, too much is left to our imagination.

1900
7 Manx and Shetland cross stock ewes
    3 × 15s to Robert Watson
    2 × 15s 6d to W. Spears
    2 × 14s to Thos. Bridson

5. Caesar Bacon with his Loghtans: the oldest known photograph of Loghtans, published in A.L.J. Gosset's book Shepherds of Britain *in 1911.*

1901
Manx ewes × 12s to 20s; ewe lambs 12s 6d to 13s

1902
5 pure Manx ewes and Manx mountain lambs
    1 ewe × £2 4s to Messrs Wilcock, Piercy, Bibaloe
    3 ewes × 28s to Mr. E.B. Gawne
    3 ewes × 22s 6d to Mr. E.B. Gawne
    Several young Manx mountain lambs made 12s to 14s 9d

1903
3 Manx ewes × £1 to Thomas Quirk
    3 Manx ewes × 17s 6d to Ben Kinvig

1904
The Manx mountain ewes fetched an average of 21s per head

1905
(No report published)

1906
    5 Manx mountain ewes × 31s 6d to Mr Christian
    5   ditto   × 26s to Mr Speedie
    5   ditto   × 17s to Mr Christian

'Pedigree rams bred by and from Mr Bacon's celebrated strain were bringing over 56s per head'

1907
Mountain ewes £1 5s and ewe lambs £1 1s

1908
Mountain ewes made £1 17s 6d

1909
Mountain ewes made 15s per head

1910
Mountain ewes made from 17s 6d to 19s

1911
'in sheep there was only a limited number'

1912
Mountain ewes made from 18s to 22s 6d
A four-horned ram sold for 20s

1913
Manx mountain ewes and lambs
    5 ewes × 25s to Geo Dalglesh
    5 ewes × 25s 6d to Michael Crowe
    6 ewes × 27s to Crowe
    5 lambs × 15s to Michael Crowe
    5 lambs × 14s 6d to Quine, Ballamoda

1914
Manx mountain ewes sold at 30s

1915
21 young Manx mountain breeding ewes and 15 ewe and wether lambs sold from 24s to £2 per head and 'were eagerly sought after'.

    Some of these buyer's names are recognisable from elsewhere. Robert Watson from Braaid was regularly winning prizes for mountain sheep at the Isle of Man Agricultural Show at this time. A ram from Thomas Bridson features in Bacon's flock book (p.10). Mr E.B. Gawne was probably his cousin, from the Gawnes of Kentraugh (*Plate 6*), whose Loghtan carriage rugs, dating

6. Caesar Bacon mounted, with the Isle of Man Hunt and members of the Gawne family at Kentraugh. about 1910. The hunt chased hares, as there are no foxes in the Isle of Man. The hunt usually managed to finish their chase at the North Star inn on the Ballamodha Straight. (Photo courtesy E.R.M. Gawne)

from the 1870s, are in the Manx Museum (p.106). It would be unwise, however, to assume that there had been Loghtans at Kentraugh throughout the intervening 30 years; and the present Mr. E.R.M. Gawne has never heard mention of Loghtans there. Ben Kinvig of Clycur had by then adopted Bacon's daughter Jane (*Plate 7*). Both Thomas Quirk and his friend Edward Christian became leading exponents of Loghtans after Bacon's death (p.28-30)[4].

The Isle of Man Agricultural Show

The list of those who won prizes at the main island show was published each year in the *Isle of Man Weekly Times*. This list could have also been a useful source of information on who else had Loghtans in Bacon's time. However, this is not the case because it seems that Loghtans could compete in a variety of classes. Some were entered as 'pure-bred mountain sheep', and in 1913 Mrs Moore of Great Meadow offered a cup for the best four-horned ram in this category. We know that they could also be entered as a 'short-wooled breed', because in 1904 'There were some very good specimens of the black-faced mountain sheep. A ram of the old Manx breed, and a four-horned one, exhibited by Mr. J.C. Bacon, attracted attention'; this had won a prize in the short-wooled class. Both the short-wooled and pure-bred mountain sheep classes had died out by 1920.

Bacon's Loghtans

Bacon wrote a piece for Gosset's book, published in 1911, as follows:

> I have a brown flock of pure Manx mountain sheep. The word loaghtan only refers to the brown colour, which is what the Shetlanders call moorit or moor-coloured. It is, however, not really the name of the breed but of the colour. Our Manx sheep are very small and finely shaped, a well-defined and handsome variety of a breed which for want of a better name I call the short-tailed sheep of Northern Europe. They were no doubt at one time wild; and on the island of Soa, one of the St. Kilda group, are still practically in a state of nature. The domestic short-tailed sheep is found pure in Iceland, the Faroe Isles, the Shetlands, Isle of Man, and a few in the Outer Hebrides, where I saw one or two good specimens this year. Probably there may still be some in the more remote Scotch highlands

7. Ben Kinvig with his wife and two sons, Stephen (left) and William (right), Florrie Faragher and Bacon's daughter Jane (seated) whom they adopted, at Clycur about 1902. Ben Kinvig kept Loghtans and bought some at Bacon's 1903 sale. (Photo courtesy of William Bealby-Wright)

and in Ireland. The breed runs in peculiar colours — white, black, brown, grey, and frequently in piebald mixtures of these colours. They have a tendency to produce four horns, and sometimes have even five or six. They are very hardy and picturesque, make excellent mutton, and except in very cold climates yield wool of exceptional quality....

He, like others of his day, treated all the short-tailed sheep of the north west as a single breed. Whether they were Soay, Manx, Hebridean, Icelandic, Shetland or Faroes sheep, they were variants of the one breed; they could be interbred but still regarded as pure short-tailed primitive sheep. This passage also shows that Bacon travelled widely and studied the sheep wherever he went.

Because Bacon described a variety of colours within the general short-tailed North European breed does not mean that he kept them all himself or indeed that all these colours were then found on the island. He said in 1911 he had a 'brown flock of pure Manx mountain sheep', and this statement is best accepted at face value. His flock was brown, and he felt able to describe them as pure even though he had imported some stock from the Shetlands. The fact that he had been selling mountain sheep in various colours at his 1904 annual sale and that by 1911 he was claiming he had a brown flock suggests that he had been culling out the other colours to create a flock of pure Loghtan-coloured sheep of the type we know today. It was probably he who established the loghtan colour as standard for the breed, using, no doubt, the moorit in the Shetlands to help with his selection programme. Most of the stock sold at his sales must have been used by others for breeding purposes, and one way or another most Loghtans today are derived from his stock, as later chapters will show.

Henry Elwes from Colesborne in Gloucestershire wrote a short article on Loghtans for the *Scottish Naturalist* after his visit to see Bacon's sheep in 1911. In this he said:

8. Head of a four-horned ram from Bacon's Seafield flock in the Manx Museum. This looks very like the ram Bacon is holding in Plate 5. (Photo by Peter Wade-Martins)

Colonel Anderson, from whose stock most of Mr. Bacon's originally came, preferred the white colour, the faces tinged with yellowish or dun, which was a common feature in the old Manx breed; but Mr Bacon as well as Mr Christian of Peel, who has a few of these sheep, prefer the loaghtan colour, and have bred for four horns, which are very well developed in some of the rams. I have now a small flock selected in the island, of which nine ewes and the old ram are loaghtan, one black, and one white with a yellowish dun face.

The brown ewes are in colour very like the Shetland *moorit* sheep, but larger, with a heavier and slightly coarser fleece. They are also distinguished by a paler topknot of wool, which in the lambs appears as a white cap. Several of my lambs, which were born black and turn brown as the wool grows, have a white tip to their tail.

The horns in the ewes are varied in form, some being curled over the top, and some curve outwards and backwards as in Black-faced ewes. This seems to be the best type of horn in the female. I saw one ewe lamb with four small but well-shaped horns. A ewe of this type is figured by Miss Gosset, p. 65. In the rams the horns are, so far as I saw, never of the Black-faced or Welsh type; but when there are four the upper ones stand high above the head or curl outwards, the secondary horns curl downwards, and sometimes grow into the sheep's cheek, or so far below his mouth that he cannot graze on short grass.

A butcher called James Brew, who had a shop in Bourne Place in Ramsey, was also said to be familiar with Bacon's stock, and described them to P.W. Caine, a member of the Manx Museum Committee, who wrote an article on the sheep in the *Isle of Man Weekly Times* in 1938:

'They are quite a nice class of sheep, but they are small, and a little slow to mature. They tend to be rather light in the bone, and their structure is what I might call goat-like....'

'Mr. Brew added that Mr Bacon used to aim at a sheep with a white spot on the face and a white point on the tail. The tails were hairy rather than woolly, and about half the ordinary length. The tails were not cut. The males had four horns, and the females two, but sometimes none.'

A ram from James Brew is on display in the Manx Museum (*Plate 29*); Billy Graham, who grew up on Staward Farm and now lives in Sulby, remembers

9. Adult ram given by Bacon in 1901 to the British Museum (Natural History). It is perhaps surprising that the ram he chose for the museum did not have a more symmetrical horn pattern. (Photo courtesy of the British Museum (Natural History))

this ram on the farm about 1935. It has a white face and an uneven set of horns, not the sort of sheep, one suspects, Bacon would have bred from, certainly not in his latter years. There is also in the museum a fine mounted four-horned ram's head given by a Mr. Kinvig (probably a descendant of Ben Kinvig) and definitely from Bacon's flock; this has a pure Loghtan colouring (*Plate 8*). The Natural History Museum in London has in store a complete Bacon ram given by him to the museum in 1901 (*Plate 9*). This ram is also a pure Loghtan.

Henry Elwes had a ram bred by Bacon in his park at Colesborne. The photograph of this ram in his *Guide to Primitive Breeds*, published in 1913, shows that it had a pure Loghtan fleece (*Plate 10*). Elwes also had other Manx stock at Colesborne by then, including a good two-horned ewe (*Plate 13*) and a white ram (*Plate 12*), no doubt all derived from the group he had assembled on the Isle of Man before writing his article for the *Scottish Naturalist* (p.17-18). The Natural History Museum has in store a two-horned Loghtan ewe without white markings presented by Elwes in 1914 (*Plate 14*).

Gosset has a photograph in her book of a painting in Bacon's possession described as a 'Loaghtan ewe and ram' (*Plate 15*). The sheep in these pictures are, as far as one can see, uniformly dark and appear to be all Loghtan, without white patches[5].

It is, therefore, doubtful whether James Brew was correct when he said in 1938 that Bacon liked Loghtans with white patches. His preference was for pure Loghtan, and it was probably Bacon's cast-offs which were reaching the butcher. White patches are, however, still part of the genetic make-up of the breed, and nearly 90 years of selective breeding has so far failed to remove them (*Plates 56 and C15*).

19

10-13. Four pictures of Manx sheep in Henry Elwes's book Guide to the Primitive Breeds of sheep and their crosses *(1913), presumably taken at his home at Colesborne in Gloucestershire. He obtained this flock during his visit to the Isle of Man in 1911.*

10. Old Manx ram bred by Caesar Bacon

11. Yearling Manx ram bred at Colesborne.

Sheep from the Faroes ?

Bacon's friend Edward Christian is reported in Caine's 1938 article as saying that because the sheep were part of the short-tailed species of north west Europe, Bacon

> '...refreshed his stock with rams from the Faroes, the Shetland Islands, and some from the Hebrides....Mr Bacon had four strains — all Manx mixed with imported sheep of the same species. He kept those strains pure, and sold them with a pedigree.'

The newspaper states that seven years before, in 1931, Bacon's steward had

12. White two-year old Manx ram

13. Manx two-horned ewe and her five-horned ram lamb.

said that Bacon had brought three ewes from the Faroes and crossed them with his original stock to produce a first cross Manx-Faroese sheep. That claim that Bacon imported ewes from the Faroes is supported in a 1931 article in the same newspaper (probably by the same author). Here it is reported that a *Times* representative had been in touch with a 'Mr. Nikkijal D. a Ryggi' from the Faroes. This man had confirmed that 'about 34 years ago' (ie in *c.* 1897) Caesar Bacon had been to the Faroes and had imported sheep from there. The article claims that Bacon imported Faroese sheep to the Isle of Man 'for the purpose of crossing them with his flock of native Manx sheep', but does not name the source. It also says that 'Mr Bacon considered that Faroes sheep gave a finer texture of wool than the Manx'.

14. Adult ewe presented by Henry Elwes in 1914 to the British Museum (Natural History). Notice the flat nose compared with the more usual shape, as in Plates 45, 65 and C13. (Photo courtesy of the British Museum (Natural History))

The author is indebted to Ulf Zachariason, research librarian at the National Library, Torshavn in the Faroes for locating the following piece by Mikkjal Danjalsson A Ryggi, published in Torshavn in 1935. This extract, translated from Faroese, is part of a description of the types of sheep found in the Faroes:

> ...Another black breed, with shorter, curlier fleece, was on Litla Dimun. These sheep were small and thin, so quick and shy that it was rarely possible to gather them all for slaughtering and it was often necessary to resort to shooting them. The meat was dark and is said to have tasted like that of game. This breed was destroyed in 1866. A few were sent to Copenhagen. and there are still three in the museum there; they are no bigger than the biggest lambs at St. Swithin's (2 July). A farmer on the Isle of Man in the Irish Sea bought three gimmers and put a ram of this breed to them there on the island. This half-Faroese breed appealed to him so much that he reared them and saw to it that they were not crossed with any other kinds. They still have them there, and they are the last remnant in existence of the oldest Faroese sheep.

Two of the specimens from Lille Dimon island in the Zoological Museum, Copenhagen were examined by Michael Ryder in 1969; he describes them in his great book on sheep where he takes the view that the breed was also a part of the northern short-tailed group. The animals are dark brown all over; the ram has two horns and the ewe is polled.

Clearly, P.W. Caine and M. Danjalsson A Ryggi had been in contact with each other about 1931, and it seems that the information from A Ryggi's article had come from Caine. How Bacon could have exported Lille Dimon sheep in the 1890s when the breed had been wiped out 30 years earlier is not explained. These stories about sheep from the Faroes all give the impression of being rather second-hand and unreliable; Caine probably never had any direct contact with Bacon who had died 15 years earlier. As 1897 was actually the year Bacon bought his seven Shetlands, probably on the same trip, the two stories could well have become confused[6].

If Bacon had used Faroes or Hebridean sheep in his breeding programme then they would surely have been entered in the flock book, which was compiled in his own hand with so much care (*Plate 3*)[7]. While it is possible that sheep were imported after his first flock book was closed in 1908, that is unlikely because by that time he had selected for the type of sheep he wanted and, as far as we know, made no more changes.

While there is no substantiated evidence that sheep from the Faroes ever reached the Isle of Man, one ram from the Isle of Man certainly did travel to the Faroes, but which breed it was we do not know. The author is grateful to Lena Nolsoe at the Faroese National Archives who has examined a report from 'The Control Committee of the Experimental Farm in Kirbjubo'. It appears that in 1896 or early in 1897 the experimental farm had imported two foreign rams, and that by April 1897 one had died from disease. The Committee was asked whether these rams were suitable to improve the local livestock. In reply on 25th April 1897 the Committee answered 'Concerning one of the imported rams, which came from the Isle of Man, we are unable to have any opinion. As for the other ram, which is of the Cheviot-race, it will probably be well fitted to improve of the faroese sheep-race...'. From the way the ram from the Isle of Man is referred to in the past tense, it seems that this was the one which had died. If rams were being imported to improve Faroese breeding stock, Bacon may well have sold the experimental farm one of his fine Shropshires

Other breeders

While Bacon undoubtedly led the way in preserving the breed in the 1890s through to his death in 1916, there were certainly other breeders as well. Henry Elwes said that when he visited the Isle of Man in 1911 Bacon had

15. The painting of a Loghtan ram and ewe as reproduced in Gosset's book Shepherds of Britain *(1911). The painting was then in Bacon's possession, but its present whereabouts is unknown. A number of photographs of the painting by D. Collister of Waverly Terrace, Douglas do, however, survive. This plate is reproduced from a copy previously in the possession of E.R.M. Gawne of Kentraugh. On the back in Bacon's own handwriting are the words 'Manx Tup and Ewe bred by J.C. Bacon, Seafield'. (Photo courtesy of Barbara Platt)*

shown him 'three of the four small flocks which exist on the island'. Entries in the flock book for rams coming into the flock and for the sale of ewes suggests that some of the following may have been the breeders Elwes had in mind: Harold Macbeth of Arragon Beg in Santon, a Miss Ponsonby, Thomas Bridson, J. Quaye and J.Q. Cannell of Ballacarnane in Michael. The names of most purchasers are not recorded in the flock book. However, we have the names of Robert Watson, W. Spears, Thomas Bridson, Wilcock and Piercy, E.B. Gawne, Thomas Quirk, Ben Kinvig (*Plate 7*), Edward Christian, Mr Speedie, George Dalglesh, Michael Crowe and a Mr Quine who bought some at the annual sales (p.15). There were certainly more flocks about, probably derived from Bacon's own stock, than Elwes realised and Bacon was prepared to admit. Few of these, however, outlasted the 1920s.

Horn numbers

Bacon says in his description of the breed that four horns were usual, but that there could be more. Elwes has a picture in his book of a fine two-horned ewe. James Brew says that Bacon's rams had four horns, his ewes two, but sometimes none. Considering the debate there is today about how many horns are acceptable, it is surprising that horn numbers were seldom noted in the past. However, there is certainly enough evidence now to show that Bacon's mountain sheep could be polled, two-horned, four-horned or even five- or six-horned.

Bacon's creation

Caesar Bacon undoubtedly saved the Manx mountain breed from extinction, but in the process he selected for the loghtan colouring he wanted at the expense of other varieties. The Manx Loghtan as we know it today was his creation from the remnants of the Manx mountain breed Robert Quirk had so stubbornly preserved. We are indebted to both men for saving the breed in an age of agricultural improvement when so many old breeds and old traditions were being swept away.

Footnotes

(1) Staward is today a 720-acre farm 5km SW of Haydon Bridge. Staward Manor is the original house, now separated from the farm with its buildings at High Staward nearby.

(2) The calculations of the size of the Shetland influence on Bacon's Loghtans were most kindly carried out by Lawrence Alderson, Technical Consultant for the R.B.S.T. Bacon also used three Lonk ewes (*Plate 3*), but their influence was found in only 5.8% of the lambs, and their overall contribution was 0.8%.

(3) The following extract from a letter by William Bealby-Wright, Bacon's grandson, to the author does more than museum documents and newspaper extracts ever can to help us understand this fascinating figure:

> The Bacons arrived in the island in the eighteenth century. They quickly integrated by marriage with established Manx families. By my grandfather's time they owned about 1000 acres in various parts of the island, all of which was managed from Seafield House. They seem to have been innovators in agriculture and built impressive farm buildings at Staward in the north, Seafield in Santon (these have been reduced considerably since the war), and Mount Murray, where they have been raised altogether. Most of these buildings were put up by his grandfather and great grandfather, one of which — I think it was his grandfather, Major Caesar Bacon — is credited with introducing turnips into the island.

> When I was a child there were still a number of people about who had worked for J.C.B. I got the impression that the livestock. including sheep, cattle (Longhorn and otherwise), game birds, boxes of rabbits, hives of bees etc. were being continuously trundled from one end of the island to the other,

not to mention commuting perpendicularly from mountain top to valley floor, in search of the best the season had to offer. The wooden ceiling of the large potting shed was entirely covered with ancient rosettes and prize cards, the seven acres of garden contained as much coke from boilers as it did soil, and scattered over it were the mysterious remains of rocky enclosures which had once housed Silver Foxes, Angora rabbits, golden pheasants, ferrets and other forgotten fauna. The house had a long-established look, lichen-covered roman stucco — not white as it is now, and much of the grandure (gilded columns etc.) has been imported recently.

My grandfather's bedroom was at the back, overlooking the farm, from which he could be raised in the morning by throwing stones at the window. He has been described as 'cultivated'. but was not a scholar, as you will have gathered from his stock book. As a youth he had to be accompanied by a posse of farm workers to the boat taking him back to Harrow at the beginning of term, and they were not allowed to return until it was well clear of the harbour, as he had a tendency to jump off it and be discovered days later at one of the farms. In later life he was well known as a judge of cattle at shows in England as well as the island.

He is also described in his obituary and other papers as 'convivial'. Much of this conviviality was enjoyed in the company of the vicar of Santon, the Reverend Jones, and these celebrations regularly ended at the Lancashire Hotel, on the main road to Douglas. Behind the Lancashire Hotel was a compound — in fact there still is — where the Highways Board kept tools and machinery; this mostly consisted of upwards of thirty wheelbarrows. Whoever was the steadier would choose a wheelbarrow and push the other home in it. I think my grandfather must have had the better head, for it was always to the vicarage lawn the Highways Board sent a waggon when they ran out of wheelbarrows.

(4) Harvey Briggs, agricultural correspondent of the *Isle of Man Examiner*, has a record that a Wilcock and Pierce were farming at Bibaloe Moar, Onchan.

(5) This painting has not survived; it was probably lost when the contents of Seafield house was dispersed, along with most of Bacon's possessions, when Teschemaker cleared the house in 1916. No estate records are known to survive either.

(6) The following extract from an article by Kenneth Williamson in *The Peregrine* in September 1945 could add weight to the case in favour of sheep from the Faroes being used in Bacon's breeding programme:

Towards the end of the last century, when he was seeking new blood to improve his Loghtyn sheep, Caesar Bacon came to the Faroes and got several animals from Kirkjubour farm. Mr Patursson tells me that his father, who was Bacon's host during his stay, afterwards received three fine Loghtyn sheep as a gift. They were put on Trollhovdi, which has very rich pasture, but unfortunately they were not used to such an exposed situation — or were too active — and were lost over the cliffs.

There are two reasons why it is difficult to accept this story. One is that it was written 50 years after the event took place. Folk memory is seldom reliable for more than one generation (ie 30 years), and, despite the detail it contains, it cannot be regarded as reliable first-hand evidence. Secondly, it is difficult to understand how Bacon would have wanted to send three good ewes to the Faroes when such breeding stock was in very short supply. By 1903/4 he had surplus stock, but not in the 1890s. It is best to discount these stories unless a reliable contemporary account can be found, in which case the issue will need to be re-examined.

It is interesting that in 1949 J.F. Robinson records in his report (p.38) that Basil Megaw was not convinced by Caine's arguments and was 'going to write to enquire about the authenticity of his statements'.

(7) A comparison between the signature on Bacon's will and the handwriting in the flock book shows that the entries are in Bacon's own handwriting.

Bacon Successors
(1916-1938)

The dispersal of Bacon's flock

Caesar Bacon died on 11th May 1916, and was buried in the family vault at Onchan church at a crowded funeral[1]. 'Universal regret prevailed ....Tradesmen, servants, peasants all proclaim Mr Bacon a real gentleman', wrote the *Isle of Man Weekly Times*. He was clearly a popular figure.

Bacon was described in his obituary in the *Manx Quarterly* for October 1916 as:

> .... an ex-president of the Isle of Man Agricultural Society, and a frequent and very successful exhibitor at the society's shows. As a scientific agriculturalist, he had a high and well deserved reputation and in this respect he ever set a good example to his fellow-farmers in the island. Among his hobbies was the breeding of long-horned cattle and of Manx mountain sheep of the old and now almost extinct strain.

Bacon was unmarried and wealthy, owning land and property in various parts of the island, especially in Santon in the south and Lezayre in the north. His farms were listed as Croft House and part of Mullen-Quinney, Ballafurt, Ballachrink (part of Ballakelly), Seafield (Santon) and Staward (Lezayre). He also had various properties in Douglas.

His sole executor was his cousin on his mother's side, William Teschemaker of Teignmouth, Devon, 'who augers well to be a worthy successor to these valuable estates'. However, an announcement of the sale of all of the livestock and equipment at the Seafield farm appeared in the same issue of *The Isle of Man Times* as the funeral report. There were two sales at Seafield, on 6th June and 18th August and one at Staward on 13th June. At Seafield most of the livestock went in the first sale, and only the poultry was held over until August. His Manx mountain sheep were entered for sale at both farms. At Seafield there were 10 ewes and lambs, four shearling ewes, three shearling rams and one '2-shearling' ram; at Staward there were 14 ewes and lambs, but no ram. So, at his death there were apparently 24 breeding ewes and four rams at his two main farms; this was not a large number, partly because he had sold 21 ewes and lambs the previous year at his annual sale (p.15).

The estate in Santon was left to William Teschemaker for his lifetime and thereafter to Isabel Jane Kinvig, the adopted daughter of Ben Kinvig of Clycur in the parish of Malew and the natural daughter of Caesar Bacon (*Plates 7 and 16*). She renounced the name of Kinvig the following year and adopted her father's name. Three years later, in 1920, Teschemaker conveyed the entire Santon property to her. Jane Bacon became a well-known Shakespearian actress and was a leading lady in the Old Vic theatre company during the years 1922-1926[2].

The Staward estate in Lezayre was left by Bacon to Teschemaker, in Trust for Joan Wilcox, who was brought up in the Teschemaker household in Devon and is believed to have been Bacon's other daughter. She seems to have followed a quieter path and married a farmer at Druidale (p.40).

16. Jane Bacon during her acting career at The Old Vic Theatre about 1926. She gave her father's Loghtan flock book (Plate 3) to the Manx Museum in 1950. (Photo courtesy of William Bealby-Wright)

Reports of the Seafield and Staward sales appeared in the *Isle of Man Weekly Times*, and the Seafield sale was long talked about as an outstanding event. Alec Maddrell, the present shepherd of the Manx Museum's Calf flock can just remember being taken there as a six-year old boy by his father.

At the 'Extraordinary Stock Sale at Seafield', the sale of the cattle and the sheep were reported upon in the newspaper, but there was, unfortunately no mention of his much-loved mountain sheep. However, the obvious quality of his pedigree cattle was widely acknowledged:

> The cattle, which were strictly pedigree longhorn, were admired by every person, several farmers frankly admitting that they had no idea such a grand stock was to be found at any one farm on the island.

All his efforts to popularise the mountain sheep had presumably met with only limited success, and their sale passed, sadly, without notice. There were no Loghtans at Seafield after 1916.

Little is recorded of what happened to the flocks of mountain sheep between 1916 and the 1930s when the evidence becomes a little clearer, but even up until the 1950s details are patchy. The memories of two people are crucial to our knowledge of the sheep in the post-Bacon era: Alec Maddrell of Port St. Mary, who shepherds the Manx Museum's Calf flock, and Bob Penrice in Oxfordshire who worked in the island's woollen mills before and after the war.

Alec Maddrell has always lived in the Port St. Mary area. He is certain that there have never been in his lifetime any flocks at the south end of the island except for the one at Strathallan, Port St. Mary; this was established by Colby Cubbin in the 1930s. He feels that the traditional home of the Loghtans was on the hills at the north end where they were valued because of their proven ability to survive in upland conditions around Sulby Glen and Glen Auldyn. Bacon's link with the breed could well, therefore, in part derive from his ownership of Staward Farm, Sulby (Lezayre), which used grazing on the hills above Sulby Glen. It seems that most of the present-day stock does originate from this area.

It is certain that until the 1970s there was only a handful of flocks with Loghtans on the island, and it is remarkable that the breed survived at all. In the period from 1925 through the 1930s Bob Penrice lived in many different parts of the island, and he never noticed Loghtans except at Sulby. He followed his father as carder and spinner first at the Tynwald Mills, then Port St. Mary and finally at Sulby Mills. The tradition was that farmers would take their wool into the mills, as Bacon did, and have it converted into cloth depending on the number of suits or other garments the farmer required. However, the Penrices saw very few Loghtan fleeces pass through the mills during their combined period of unbroken service from 1916 to 1956.

Bacon's successors: Quirk, Cannell and Christian

The only record of the purchasers of Bacon's flock in 1916 is in the two articles by P.W. Caine, written for the *Isle of Man Weekly Times*. The first was published in January 1931:

> (The wearing of suits of Loghtan cloth) is still kept up by Mr. J.T. Quirk, Ballacosnahan, Patrick, who bought from Mr. Bacon's flock. Mr. Quirk still breeds the sheep, as do various farmers in the North of the island — for Mr. Bacon owned the farms at Staward and Ballabrooie, at Sulby, and grazed these sheep there. After his death his stock was sold by auction, and among other purchasers of this flock of sheep was the late Colonel Moore. The cloth was sometimes mixed with a few black fleeces from the original unimproved Manx stocks.

The only photograph of Loghtans known to survive from the 1920s is actually of a ram belonging to Mr. Quirk of Ballacosnahan in Patrick taken in February 1924 (*Plate 17*). It is a four-horned ram with light areas to either side of the nose. This breeder is probably the same as the Thomas Quirk who bought three ewes at Bacon's 1903 annual Seafield sale. J.T. Quirk and Mrs Moore won prizes for their Manx sheep at the Southern Agricultural Show from 1924 to 1926 (p.81).

The second was published in October 1938:

> But so far as we can ascertain, all surviving loaghtan sheep came from Mr. Bacon's flocks. The late Mr. J.Q. Cannell of Ballacarnane, Michael, who was a close friend of Mr. Bacon's, had some loaghtan sheep, which he crossed with the Cheviot; the late Mr. Robert Fayle, of Ballabrooie, Lezayre, went into a farm which belonged to Mr. Bacon till his death; and it is understood that loaghtans belonging to Mr. J. T. Quirk, Ballacosnahan, Patrick, Mr. E.T. Christian, Ballacallin, Patrick, and Mrs Lascelles of Maughold, were acquired from the same source. Mr. Bacon used to have a big sheep sale every year.

and later in the same article:

> Many people will remember the light brown suits which Mr. Bacon wore, and what a picturesque figure he made in them. They were all cut from cloth made from the loaghtan wool. Mr J.Q. Cannell was similarly attired, and so was Mr J.T. Quirk when the present writer saw him some months ago.

17. A two-year old Manx ram belonging to Thomas Quirk a Ballacosnahan, dated February 1924. (Photo courtesy of the Manx Museum)

Edward Christian

E.T.Christian, a Peel bank manager and farmer, had a flock of about 30 Loghtans at Ballacallin, Patrick, for many years. He was quoted in 1938 in the *Isle of Man Weekly Times*:

'My own stock was getting very small,' he told a 'Times' representative, 'until three years ago I got two rams from Sir Buchanan Jardine, of Glasgow, whose estate, if I remember correctly, is in Dumfriesshire. They were exactly the same species as my own — that is to say, they were short-tailed sheep of Northern Europe.'....

'I have had loaghtan sheep for about fifty years,' Mr Christian said. 'I got them, like other people for the sake of a rarity, and in order to keep something that was Manx still alive'

But Mr. Christian is enthusiastic about these sheep on their own merits. They make very good mothers; their meat has an excellent flavour, and their wool is as fine as that from Shetland. Also, it lasts and lasts.

'Mr. Bacon had an overcoat of loaghtan wool which he wore for thirteen years. Then he gave it to a man in Sulby. Four or five years later he bought it back again, and he declared it was in better condition than before!'

Not long ago Lady Butler, wife of the last Governor, had a costume made from loaghtan wool supplied by Mr Christian.'

Christian gave up farming in 1942 and moved to Northop, Greeba, with a small flock of Loghtans. From there he wrote to Sir Mark Collet in September 1943:

I am afraid the Loughtan strain is likely to become extinct in the Island very shortly, owing to the difficulty of procuring unrelated rams. The breed had nearly died out a few years ago, but I got, at a Royal Show, from (a) Scotch shepherd, the information that Sir Buchanan-Jardine kept some of this colour at his country estate. I got a ram from this gentleman and was enabled to bring my flock up to standard again.

Having given up farming in a largish way last November, my flock was dispersed, to a certain extent; I have now only got 15 ewes left, but am without a Loughtan ram, and as there is not a large quantity of land connected with Northop House there is no chance of running a decent flock so as to make it worth while importing rams.

In order to perpetuate the breed in the Island Mr. Bacon persuaded a few farmers and myself to run a small flock, and during his lifetime we were able to acquire suitable rams from him, but after his death this supply was cut off and the smaller flocks thus died out. As I had a larger number I was able to carry on longer and my flock got smaller by the year until I got Sir Buchan Jardine's ram and so built my flock up again.'

It therefore appears that Quirk, Cannell and Christian were the men who saw themselves as successors to Bacon and did their best to promote the breed after his death through the 1920s and 1930s.

Mrs Moore of Great Meadow

There were also two ladies who played a leading role in the story at this time. Mrs Moore at Great Meadow near Castletown had a flock of 20 or so, including, no doubt, those bought by Colonel Moore at Bacon's dispersal sale. Mrs Moore presented a cup for the best four-horned ram at the Isle of Man Agricultural Show in 1913 (p.81) and a set of silver flower vases for the best pen of Manx sheep at the Southern Agricultural Show, in 1924 (*Plate 75*). Lt. Colonel R.H.D. Riggall, her grandson who lives at Great Meadow, remembers her Loghtan flock, and Mrs Riggall (as she was later called) gave a ram's skull to the Manx Museum in 1936/7 (*Plate 18*).

18. A skull of a four-horned ram in the Manx Museum from a flock belonging to Mrs Moore at Great Meadow, near Castletown. Mrs Moore did much to promote the breed during the decade after Bacon's death. (Photo by Peter Wade-Martins)

Mrs Lascelles

The next was Mrs Lascelles who had a flock of 34 Loghtans at Maughold up until 1938; then her flock was reduced when she moved to 'Willow Dene', St. Jude's Road, Sulby. Her foundation stock of ewes had been given to her by a Mr. Quirk, presumably Thomas Quirk, in about 1933. To start with she used a ram belonging to Robert Fayle 'which seemed to be the only ram on the island'. Later, she used two rams from Edward Christian 'who received them from a gentleman in Dumfries, who had the breed for many years and had kept it pure'. These were the two rams Edward Christian imported from the Castlemilk estate near Lockerbie in Dumfriesshire in 1936 (p.93).

So, Mrs Lascelles's flock was of Bacon's stock via Thomas Quirk. The ram she used to start with — Robert Fayle's — was at Ballabrooie, on a farm in Lezayre'which belonged to Mr Bacon', in other words, Staward. One way or another, all her stock originated from Bacon's except for the one or two imported Castlemilk rams kept at Ballacallin.

A stuffed lamb from her flock is on display in the Manx Museum. Most of her stock went to another Mr Quirk at Ballanayre, German, and she gave two ewes to the island's Knockaloe Experimental Farm.

The Manx Museum has a copy of a 1946 survey of Loghtan flocks in the Isle of Man carried out for the museum by G. Wyllie Howie, Agricultural Organiser for the I.o.M. Board of Agriculture, which shows that Mrs Lascelles still had 10 ewes then, although there is no record of when or how she finally gave up shepherding[3].

Ballawattleworth and Ballaquaggin
Finally, there is a ewe's head in the Manx Museum (*Plate 19*), donated in 1934 and said to have been bred by an F.W. Quirk at Ballawattleworth, but no further information on his flock survives. We also know that Reggie Quirk at Ballaquaggin had Loghtans and competed with them at the Southern Agricultural Show (p.81).

The success of Bacon's annual sales
One is struck by the fact that during the post-Bacon years it was the number of people with a few sheep which kept the breed alive. This was entirely due to the fact that stock had been widely distributed on the island through Bacon's annual sales. Perhaps more than any other factor, this ensured the breed's survival during the inter-war period. However, 20 years after his death the situation was clearly becoming critical once more.

Footnotes
(1) The Bacon vault is the large house-like structure opposite the west end of Onchan church.

(2) In 1926 Jane Bacon married George Bealby-Wright, a West End actor who died in 1931. As Mrs Bealby-Wright she returned to Seafield in 1939. During the difficult war years she maintained Seafield house and gardens single handed, and for some time farmed Ballafurt farm nearby with one man and two horses. By 1945 this had become too much for her, and Seafield house and the farm were sold together with Ballafurt. As she left Seafield she wrote the following moving piece in her diary:

> ...and said farewell. The great house was swept and cleared, not a scrap or stick left to mar it. It stood in the red sunset, cleared of all tawdry human rubbish that had lately so troubled and degraded it. It stood nobly alone, looking on the sea and flaming sky and flooded with the red glory of sunset.

Jane Bealby-Wright died in 1981 at the age of 85.

(The author is grateful to William Bealby-Wright, Bacon's grandson, for explaining the complexities of the Bacon succession.)

(3) This survey is covered by the ruling of the Director of the Manx Museum that internal museum documents are not open to inspection by researchers (p.61). However, Dr. Larch Garrad at the museum assures the writer that there is nothing else in the survey which he has not picked up from other sources.

C1. Air photograph of Seafield (or Arragon House as it is called today). To the right of the house are the farm buildings used by Bacon; the meadow behind and to the right is where his annual livestock sales were held until 1913. (Photo courtesy of Manx Technical Publications)

C2. Seafield house and lawns, described in Bacon's day as 'quite an Elysium, commanding every comfort with exceptional scenery'. (Photo by Peter Wade-Martins)

C3. The Bacon crest and the date 1842 over the entrance to the Staward farm buildings. (Photo by Peter Wade-Martins)

C4. *Ballamanaugh, Sir Mark Collet's mansion built in 1936, with Primrose Hill (or Cronk Sumark) behind. (Photo by Peter Wade-Martins)*

C5. *The hills above Sulby Glen, the traditional home of the Manx mountain sheep, with Druidale Farm in the distance. (Photo by Peter Wade-Martins)*

C6. Loghtans on the rocky cliffs of the Calf of Man overlooking the Irish Sea. (Photo by Peter Wade-Martins)

C7. Loghtans in the fields near the old farmhouse on the Calf, now occupied by staff of the Bird Observatory. (Photo by Alex Maddrell)

C8. Left. A ram being clipped during the annual round-up on the Calf. (Photo by Alex Maddrell)

C9. Below. A boatload of Loghtan lambs leaving the Calf in 1980. (Photo by Alex Maddrell)

C10. A Loghtan ewe and her lamb at the Cregneash folk museum one misty morning in 1988. (Photo by Peter Wade-Martins)

Sir Mark Collet and Colby Cubbin (1938-1953)

Sir Mark Collet

Numbers were becoming precariously low again in the late 1930s. This time the breed was saved by a retired farmer from Kent, who stepped in just in time as Caesar Bacon had done before him. Sir Mark Collet was the son of Sir Mark Wilks Collet, merchant banker and Director of the Bank of England from 1866 and Governor of the Bank from 1887 to 1889. He graduated from Cambridge with a law degree in 1885, but was never called to the bar. He succeeded his father as a baronet in 1905 and was High Sheriff of Kent in 1912 and an Alderman from 1925 to 1936. He was a J.P. and chairman of Kent Education Committee for 11 years from 1921 (*Plate 20*). Nevertheless, he managed to combine public life with farming on his estate at Kemsing in Kent, having a prize-winning herd of shorthorns. A surviving County show catalogue for 1923, preserved by the Kent County Agricultural Society, records five Dairy Shorthorn entries from him in that year. In 1935, when he was 71, he moved to the Isle of Man where he built a large house for himself at Ballamanaugh in Sulby in 1936 (*Plate 21*). During the nine years he lived on the island he devoted much of his energies to supporting Ramsey hospital for which he was an investment trustee. He died at Ballamanaugh on 24 September 1944.

20. A caricature of Sir Mark Collet published in The Kent Messenger *in 1932 at the time of his retirement as chairman of the Kent Education Committee.*

33

21. Ballamanaugh, built by Sir Mark Collet in Sulby in 1936. (Photo by Peter Wade-Martins)

Sir Mark gathered together most of the remaining sheep, and they grazed for a while on Primrose Hill (Cronk Sumark) close by his new mansion (*Plate C4*). Unfortunately, no records of the flock survive, and when the Manx Museum took possession of the flock from his widow in 1953 little information about its origins or its management came with them. The Museum records apparently show that Chrystals, the Ramsey auctioneers, bought in Sir Mark's sheep for him, no doubt because they had better contacts around the local farms than Sir Mark did. It is tempting to assume that they were from Edward Christian and Mrs Lascelles, supplemented, perhaps, by a few others from the Sulby area. The flock was certainly not assembled until after 1938, the year Mrs Lascelles reduced her flock. It numbered 25-30 animals in 1945 and about 35 in 1952. Only one useful photograph of them (*Plate 22*) is known to survive from the period prior to their transfer to the Museum. Man was very depressed in the 1930s; cameras were scarce, and from 1939 to 1945 film was virtually unobtainable.

Sir Mark had collected the sheep because he was fascinated with Manx heritage, believing his family to be descended from the Corletts of Ballaugh. He was also instrumental in saving Spanish Head, near the Calf of Man, for the Manx National Trust, and he particularly wanted to see Loghtans on the Calf.

In about 1940, the sheep were handed over to John (Willie) Dale, a butcher in Douglas Street, Peel, to look after. They were put on Peel Hill, overlooking Peel Castle, and they stayed there until the Manx National Trust accepted them in 1953.

The Agricultural Organiser of the Isle of Man Board of Agriculture Knockaloe Experimental Farm, G. Wyllie Howie, assisted with the management of the flock, but he was obviously not over enthusiastic about Loghtans; he wrote in November 1945 to a correspondent in Glasgow one of the few contemporary accounts of the flock at that period:

> There are still some of the old Manx (Loughtan) breed left. We have 5 of them on this farm, but they are now somewhat elderly. The Late Sir Mark Collett collected a flock of these sheep, which now numbers about 25 — 30. At the moment they are being grazed on some rough ground near Peel. There are a few other scattered remnants of the breed throughout the Island, but they are not kept on any large scale, and their economic importance is almost negligible.

There is only one short piece written by Sir Mark about his sheep (in words which closely echo those in the letter he had received two years earlier from Edward Christian quoted in part on p.30). This piece was published posthumously in *The Countryman* for Autumn 1945, and was reprinted in the *Isle of Man Courier* in January 1946. In this he said:

22. *Loghtans at Peel Castle in the 1940s (Photo courtesy of Mr. J.F. Robinson)*

> The mountain sheep were not kept pure by the lowland farmers, as they had then gone in for the larger breeds. There would occasionally be a few Manx sheep in their flocks, but they were either black or white. I do not remember any Loughtans among them. The small Manx sheep, as a flock, were confined to the hill-men....
>
> Both rams and ewes have horns: one line of Mr Bacon's — he kept three private flock registers — had two horns; another had an uncertain number. I have seen three, four and five, but this lot's horns were really symmetrical.
>
> I find the Loughtan colour is not dominant like the black colour. I have many times mated a Loughtan ram with white ewes, and vice versa, but have never had a lamb of Loughtan colour in the issue. I am afraid the Loughtan strain is likely to become extinct in the island very shortly, owing to the difficulty of procuring unrelated rams. The breed had nearly died out a few years ago, but I had, at a Royal Show, from Scotch shepherds, the information that Sir Buchanan Jardine kept some of this colour and I got a ram from him.

Sir mark's crossing experiments presumably refer to the fact that if one crosses a Loghtan with an ordinary white commercial sheep, the distinctive colour rarely comes through in the offspring. Clearly, he felt that the survival of the Loghtan colour was crucial for the survival of the breed. His importation of another Castlemilk ram from Scotland shows that the perpetuation of the moorit colour was his over-riding priority, as it had been for Edward Christian before him.

The report of the Animal Breeding and Genetic Research Organisation

The flock at Peel was visited in May 1949 by Mr. J.F. Robinson of the Animal Breeding and Genetics Research Organisation who was then engaged in a comprehensive survey of British breeds of sheep. His report on the flock was never published, but luckily he has kept the typescript in his possession ever since. This report, covering 11 foolscap pages, describes the flock in some detail and lists all the rams used during the 1940s.

In 1949 there were 19 ewes, all two-horned except two with four horns, 25 lambs and a ram. The hill was not well fenced and the flock roamed quite freely in and out of their fenced area. 'The sheep are fairly wild and could not be examined at close quarters...They are in fact a great nuisance to all the neighbours.' Six of the ewes were shearlings sired by a powerful two-horned 'Shetland' ram said to have been slaughtered in 1947 after it had killed two neighbour's rams 'at a stroke'. The ram and the shearling ewes had a 'reversed badger face pattern' not seen on the older ewes. (This term was used at the time amongst geneticists to describe a dark face with light areas around the eyes and mouth as found on Soay and Mouflon sheep). Previous to that, Lady Collet had used a four-horned ram from Mr. W. Cannell of Ballacarnane, Michael.

Mr. Robinson understood that the only other flocks on the island by that time belonged to Mrs. Lascelles and a Walter Quirk of Peel. The ram then with the flock, probably that in *Plate 22*, had been purchased from Walter Quirk.

On receiving the report, Professor R.G. White, of the A.B.G.R.O. submitted the following advice on the best method of preserving the breed to the Manx Museum and to Lady Collet.

From his (Mr. Robinson's) report, and from other accounts of the breed (notably Lydekker's book on 'The Sheep and its Cousins'), it seems fairly certain that the Manx breed is one branch of the Short Tailed sheep which occurred at one time over many parts of Great Britain, and Northern Europe, and still survive with various modifications in the Shetlands, Faroe and some Scandinavian Islands. Lady Collett's flock appears in fact to contain the blood of importations both from the Faroes and the Shetlands. It, therefore, probably contains no genetic constituent which could not be obtained from other sources.

Maintenance of the flock thus appears to have been justified mainly on historical and sentimental grounds.

From Mr. Robinson's report, I gather that it would not be difficult to maintain the flock on present lines, especially as the recent introduction of a Shetland ram has added vigour to the flock as a whole. If a brown son of his is kept for breeding purposes, he could be used on the off-spring of the three year old Loghtan ram, and similarly ewe lambs from the Shetland ram might be mated to the old ram himself. In this way, by ringing the changes on the two lines, excessive inbreeding can be avoided for a number of generations, provided that two rams are always kept, and that the ewes are mated to the ram which is less closely related to them. To be perfectly safe, it would be well to keep more than one ram of each line so as to have a reserve in case of accidents or deaths. The chief difficulty would appear to be the keeping of more rams than one, as I gather that the sheep range over a big hill, and there might be difficulty in separating the two lots at tupping time.

It seems unfortunate that the Shetland ram was not of the whole brown colour which the majority of the Loghtan sheep possess, because many of the Shetland rams are of this colour. The pattern which has been introduced will, however, soon disappear if the rams selected for breeding are all of the same usual brown colour.

23-8. The following six pictures by Kenneth Whitehead are of the Manx Museum's flock at Druidale taken in June 1953. Note the light markings around the mouth and eyes of the ram and also down the inside of the legs of the ewes and lambs. In Plate 26 the white belly and white area around the tail of the lamb is prominent. These markings are typical of what are now called Castlemilk Moorit sheep, as shown on Plates 87-91 and C21. (Photos by Kenneth Whitehead)

23-4. A two-horned ram probably imported by, or the son of a ram imported by, Sir Mark Collet from Sir John Buchanan-Jardine's Castlemilk estate near Lockerbie in Dumfriesshire.

Castlemilk rams

The imported ram was not actually pure Shetland. It was a two-horned moorit-coloured sheep from Sir John (or Jock) Buchanan- Jardine's Castlemilk estate near Lockerbie in Dumfriesshire *Plate 86*). Sir John had in the 1930s created the Castlemilk Shetland breed, or the Castlemilk Moorit as it is known today, and Edward Christian's earlier imported ram or rams were from the same flock. After Sir John died in November 1969, most of this unique flock was slaughtered the following year, except for a handful which Joe Henson saved for the Cotswold Farm Park. Recent research into the origin and make-up of this breed is set out in a later chapter (p.92-95).

There is some doubt about whether the troublesome 'Shetland' ram had in fact been slaughtered in 1947, because Professor White talks as though it ought to be possible to keep one of his sons. When the flock was transferred to the ownership of the Manx National Trust in 1953, a ram of similar type and temperament was still with the flock. This came to a sticky end, as Major Brownsdon wrote to Kenneth Whitehead in August 1953:

> So far as I can gather, the Loghtan ram did come from Sir Buchanan-Jardine's place at Lockerbie; at any rate, it did come from outside the island, as Sir Mark Collet, who got the flock together, was worried about excessive inbreeding. As you note, the ram is no more; he killed one of my best Scots Blackface rams in a fight but met his end when he tried some tricks on an old Clydesdale mare, with whom he was sharing the field.

This ram (or more likely his son) had been photographed by Kenneth Whitehead (*Plates 23-4*) during his visit to the island in June of that year while he was preparing an article on Loghtans for *Country Life*. Because of this lucky timing, we have an excellent record of the appearance of the ram which clearly had a major input into the genetic make-up of the flock from the 1940s up until 1953. It appears that Lady Collet did not take Professor White's advice to maintain two bloodlines, and used only one ram because of the difficulties of maintaining separate tupping groups on Peel Hill. The Castlemilk Moorit breed today is two-horned in both sexes; the face is brown with lighter markings under the jaw, around the eyes, around the tail, on the belly and down the inside of the legs (*Plates 88-91 and C21-2*). These areas of lighter colouring, so typical of the Soay, are obvious in Kenneth Whitehead's pictures, less so in the ram, but clearly in his offspring (*Plates 25-8*). Presumably, this is why Professor White said it was unfortunate that the ram 'was not of the whole brown colour'.

There were, however, other flocks on the island, a fact not fully appreciated by Professor White when he said that because the breed was so influenced by imported stock its maintenance was only justified 'on historical and sentimental grounds.'

In 1945 Lady Collet had offered the English National Trust the opportunity of having the flock to run on the Calf, but this offer was refused because of the problems of shepherding them. However, it was accepted by the Manx Museum and National Trust in 1953: a decision which ensured the survival of the breed.

Colby Cubbin

There were at least two further flocks of Loghtans on the island which were maintained through the 1950s, unknown to the Manx Museum staff who believed in 1953 that Lady Collet's flock represented all that remained of the Loghtans at that time. There were one or two near Sulby and the other was at Strathallan Castle, Port St. Mary. The history of the Strathallan flock is well recorded.

25. Ewes and lambs.

26. A ewe (left) and lamb with two wethers.

27. A wether.

28. A ewe.

Strathallan has a fascinating history. The house was built in 1895 by Dr. Jotham on the cliffs at Port St. Mary at a spot known as Shag Rock. Ellen Cubbin, from Strathallan Cliff, Onchan, bought it from Jotham's widow in 1933 and re-named it Strathallan Castle. She was wealthy, and all her properties, including a steam yacht in Port St. Mary harbour, were called Strathallan. The house was used mainly by her son Colby, who was a bachelor, an eccentric, and a radio ham; he began a flock of Loghtans in the fields around the house, probably in the 1930s, although the date and the origins of the flock are not recorded.

Colby Cubbin died in 1955, followed by his mother later the same year. Her executors then offered the '18 Loghtan and other cross sheep and one ram' to the Manx Museum. When the museum declined they passed to Nellie Keig, Colby Cubbin's housekeeper. The later history of the flock will be covered in a subsequent chapter (p.58-61).

The Fayles at Staward Farm

It seems that all the successors to Bacon kept Loghtans at Staward, or Ballabrooie as it was still sometimes called. Bacon left the farm to Joan Wilcox then living in Newton Abbot in Devon who later married a Captain W. Wilson of Druidale. She then rented Staward for a while to Richard Cain, a Castletown brewer, but sold it in 1922 to Robert Fayle, who we know from P.W. Caine's 1938 article had Loghtans. Robert Fayle had three sons, John, Tommy and Jimmy who continued to run the farm. Jimmy is the only surviving brother, and he is now over 90 and still living in the farmhouse, although the farm was sold in 1986 to Dr McDonald at Ballamanaugh. The brothers had a flock of about 30 Loghtans which they knew were descended from Bacon's stock (*Plates 29-30*). This they supplemented in the early 1940s with Loghtans from William Crowe's dispersal sale at Balladoole, near Ramsey. The Fayles gave them up during the last war when they literally lost them. One day their Loghtans escaped from some grazing land rented near Druidale and were last seen heading towards Kirk Michael. Despite searches the Fayles never saw their Loghtans again!

While the Staward sheep have long since gone, some of their wool survives. In 1933 a load of Loghtan fleeces was put in the loft over one of the stables at Staward by Robert Fayle. This was discovered recently, and enough of the wool, now more than 50 years old, remained in good order for it to be hand spun and knitted into a pullover for Jack Quine (*Plate C17*).

There are some undated, but presumably pre-war photographs in the Manx Museum of two rams on the meadow behind Sulby School which was part of Staward land (*Plate 30*).

29. A ram with four horns and a white face, probably from Staward, in the Manx Museum donated by James Brew, a Ramsey Butcher in 1937. (Photo by Keig, 1943; courtesy of the Manx Museum)

Ballacaley

Also in Sulby is Ballacaley Farm where the Kneale brothers farmed until the 1980s (*Plates 31-2*). Andy, the younger brother, died in 1978 and Fred in 1986, aged 82. These brothers, Jack Quine remembers, had many different breeds and 'were always keen on trying something new'. They were 'criss-crossing them all ways' and no breed seemed to remain pure for long. Nevertheless, there was still one last pure-bred ram on the farm in 1975 which was bought by Ken Briggs and taken back to his rare breeds farm in Worcestershire. It was registered in the Combined Flock book in 1975 as '921' and was used to sire all his 1976 lambs. So, despite the Kneale's crossing experiments, some pure breeding continued on the farm throughout the 1950s and 1960s.

Local memory does not now record whether the Ballacaley flock was an ancient one, but there was a long-held tradition amongst some farmers in the Sulby area of keeping a few Loghtans almost for good luck. All we know is that Ballacaley was bought by Andy and Fred's father, William Kneale, about 1908 when he erected new farm buildings. The farm buildings have just recently been pulled down, but the house remains.

30. An undated picture of a pair of rams at Staward Farm on the meadow behind Sulby school. This must date to sometime before the Fayles literally lost their Staward flock of Loghtans on the hills near Druidale during the last war. *(Photo courtesy of the Manx Museum)*

31. Andy Kneale with two rams at Ballacaley in 1957. *(Photo courtesy of Lewis Barham)*

32. The Ballacaley flock in 1957 showing pure and cross-bred stock, with Andy Kneale behind. The two four-horned ewes in the centre foreground seem to be exhibiting some Castlemilk markings on face and legs. (Photo courtesy of Lewis Barham)

The Kneale brothers told Ken Briggs in 1975 that their father had exported some Loghtans to the Castlemilk estate in Scotland 1930s, as did the Manx Museum in 1955 (p.47). Plate 32 shows the Ballacaley flock in 1957 with at least two of the ewes showing Castlemilk markings, so the Kneales seem to have had the use of one of the imported rams at some stage.

The Situation in 1953

By 1953 the Loghtans on the island were apparently down to three known flocks. Lady Collet had 35 on Peel Hill, Colby Cubbin had about 18 (including some crossbreds) at Strathallan, Port St. Mary and the Kneale brothers had an unknown, but probably small, number at Ballacaley, Sulby. There may have been a few in unrecorded flocks, but the island total was probably well under 100 in the early 1950s. It is doubtful that there was any pure-bred stock still surviving on the hills, although there were still some black unimproved cross-breds about. No pure-bred flocks are recorded from outside the island at this time.

During the period covered in this chapter there were two moments when the breed could easily have become extinct. One was in the late 1930s and early 1940s when breeders like Edward Christian and Mrs Lascelles were giving up. If a flock of animals had not been pulled together then by Sir Mark Collet, it is unlikely that the breed would have survived. Again, in the early 1950s when it seemed nobody wanted that same flock then on Peel Hill, the Manx Museum's decision to take it over was crucial. While there were other flocks available on both occasions, it is unlikely that their numbers were sufficient or their breeders well enough organised to retrieve the situation by themselves.

The Manx Museum

The Museum takes over

The Manx Museum and National Trust became owners of Lady Collet's flock on 27th March 1953. The flock had consisted of 'over 30' animals. Although numbers were already low, and the professional staff in the Museum were not aware of the Strathallan or Ballacaley flocks, only 12 ewes and a ram were retained, leaving half a dozen with John Dale on Peel Hill; the fate of the remaining dozen is not recorded.

The museum left the management of the sheep to Major T.E. Brownsdon, a museum trustee, who lived at Ballalough, West Baldwin (*Plate 33*). In early March he transferred the 12 sheep to the Baldwin Valley in time for lambing. By May they had reached Druidale Farm at the top of the Sulby Glen; there they remained for the next 25 years under the care of Jack Quine (*Plate 37*), farm manager for Captain G.H. Drummond, the owner, and Major Brownsdon, who farmed it in partnership with him.

We know the size of the Druidale flock in June because Kenneth Whitehead records in the article he wrote for *Country Life* that there were then 12 ewes with 17 lambs. Jack Quine remembers that during the latter years the sheep were on Peel Hill they became rather neglected; they were often escaping and found wandering the streets of Peel. As a result, many of the ewes had been crossed with other rams and the number of pure-bred stock in the group was declining. Whether the apparent culling from 30 to 12 was an attempt to weed out cross-bred stock or whether the museum only wanted to be responsible for 12 ewes is not clear; however, it did bring the numbers precariously low.

We have an excellent record of the flock as it looked that summer at Druidale Farm, thanks to the photography of Kenneth Whitehead. On receiving a set of prints, the Director of the Museum, Basil Megaw, wrote to Kenneth Whitehead that August saying 'They are certainly the best photos I have ever seen of our Manx sheep', as indeed they were. The set is reproduced in full (*Plates 23-8*) because it is such an excellent record of some of the animals in the main flock at the time, and because the pictures record how much the Castlemilk ram and its predecessors had affected the appearance of what remained of Lady Collet's stock.

Kenneth Whitehead's photographs show the ram (killed the next month by Major Brownsdon's Clydesdale horse), some of the ewes, which were mainly two-horned, with their lambs and some four-horned wethers. The light Castlemilk markings are clear on the ewes and even more so on their lambs. As the ram had been used since Sir Mark Collet's time, it had probably sired many of the ewes as well as their lambs and the flock must have become very inbred.

The flock has no ram

After the ram died, Basil Megaw's secretary wrote to Kenneth Whitehead in early August for advice on where to obtain another ram.

> '...we should be glad if you have any ideas as to whom we should approach in replacing this animal. We do not know of any other pure-bred Loghtan rams on the Island, and think that this one had been imported from Galloway (Sir Buchanan Jardine) by the former owner of our flock (the late Sir Mark Collet).

33. Major T.E. Brownsdon,
1980. He help the Manx
Museum preserve the breed by
providing space for the
museum flock at Druidale
Farm from 1953 to 1977.
*(Photo courtesy of Mrs Margaret
Brownsdon)*

Kenneth Whitehead replied

I imagine that the ram was the one I saw on Major Brownsdon's farm and I was much struck by its similarity to a Shetland ram I saw a few weeks earlier. If, therefore, this ram, as is suggested in your letter originally was imported from Sir Buchanan Jardine's flock in Scotland then this would confirm that it was a pure Shetland for it was his flock that I had visited.

He suggested that they should either import another Castlemilk ram from Scotland or try 'a very nice four horned ram lamb on the farm at Sulby which Mr. Howie took me to see....It was a very good specimen and may well be the last of the four horned on the island..' Kenneth Whitehead didn't gather the Sulby farmer's name, but it was almost certainly one of the Kneale brothers at Ballacaley. This advice was passed on to Major Brownsdon, but it is frustrating that nobody can now remember which option was chosen. However, several photographs taken of the museum flock in 1955 (*Plates 34-6*) show the flock with a four-horned ram which suggests that the the Sulby ram was used.

Management of the flock remained in Major Brownsdon's hands, and there was an agreement between the museum and Major Brownsdon that the numbers should never drop below 12 animals and that he could keep surplus stock

34. The ram, probably from the Ballacaley flock.

35. The 11 ewes with the ram at the back. The ewe that went to London Zoo may be the one to right of centre in the foreground (See Plate 38).

and the wool in return for their keep. For most of the next 25 years, management of the flock was in practice left to Jack Quine who lived at the farm (*Plate 37*). The Loghtans were run with the farm's hill flock, except at tupping, although for most of the time they usually kept to themselves and grazed in a group. While he regarded the Loghtans as a 'dead loss' in commercial terms, he tried to keep the breed going despite the lack of support he received

at the time. As Jack often says when recalling this period, 'Nobody was really that interested.' No breeding records were ever kept by the museum, but he is sure that the flock was always bred pure except for occasional accidents.

Whipsnade Zoo
The first sheep to contribute to the present population of Loghtans in Britain left the island in 1955, and a photograph of the event was published on the front page of the *Isle of Man Examiner* on 20th May (*Plate 38*). The group, consisting of a ram, two ewes and their lambs, went to London Zoo. Only one female (probably an original lamb) and her lamb remained when the flock was moved to Whipsnade in 1959. She died of old age at Whipsnade in 1963. The two ewes from London Zoo were made up into a breeding group by the purchase of a ram from a Mr. Vondy in October 1961. The Zoo's correspondence with Mr Vondy was lost in an office fire in 1962, but the Curator believes the ram came from the Isle of Man; this was almost certainly Leslie Vondy who was then Estate Agent for Captain Drummond. It was this ram and six of his offspring (three rams and three ewes) which were transferred to the National Agricultural Centre at Stoneleigh in October 1968.

Sheep to Castlemilk
One of Jack Quine's old calendars shows that on 15th November 1955, sheep went to the Castlemilk estate in Scotland, but how many and for what purpose is not recorded. Documents relating to this transfer have recently been found in the Castlemilk estate office (p.94).

Numbers dwindle: vaccines save the day
In the early years Jack did not have much success with the Loghtans. The change of scene for the flock from sea level to a hill farm with land rising to almost 1,500 feet, had a devastating effect on numbers. On top of that, the lambs seemed to do well until weaning, but then they often died. He never

37. Jack Quine at Grange Farm, Sulby, 1987. He was farm manager at Druidale from 1947 to 1977. We owe the survival of the breed to his unceasing efforts during the 1950s and 1960s at a time when numbers were so critically low. (Photo by Peter Wade-Martins)

38. A ram, ewe and lamb, part of the group exported from the museum flock to London Zoo in May 1955, outside the shipping office of the Isle of Man Steam Packet building. Holding the sheep are left to right: steam packet clerk, Jack Quine and a journalist. (Photo Isle of Man Examiner; courtesy of the Manx Museum)

knew the reason for this, but suspected that the heavy doses of lime (2 tons/acre) he was spreading on the farm to reclaim the moorland and to improve the grazing was the cause. Photographs show that there were 11 ewes in 1955 (Plates 35-6), but numbers dwindled lower to seven ewes and a ram by 1956. He was at a loss to know what to do, and no advice he received seemed to make any difference. Not only are there no museum breeding records; there are no details of flock numbers either, so precise information on how the size of the flock fluctuated between 1953 and 1972 in not now available[1].

Just when the flock was at the point of extinction sheep vaccines were introduced on the farm. In 1958 the Loghtan flock, along with the rest of the sheep on Druidale Farm, were injected; then, to Jack's surprise, he had no further deaths. Slowly, the situation improved, helped by the fact that the next generation was acclimatised to the hills. Flock numbers are not recorded, but gradually it was possible to pass stock on to other breeders, first on the island and then in England and in Scotland.

Soay ram

In 1966 the Manx Museum decided to buy in a Soay ram lamb from Monks Wood Experimental Station near Huntingdon to cross with some of the ewes to strengthen the flock. This ram arrived in October; it was used for one mating season and died from a massive worm infestation the following February. The decision to import the Soay was one which Jack afterwards regretted because the breeds were so different. However, all the ewe lambs from the one season were kept for breeding, but the males were culled. Monks Wood offered another ram, but the offer was not taken up, and Jack reverted to his existing Loghtan rams for the next year.

Later, in 1973 or 1974 any descendants of the ram with very prominent Soay markings in the flock which Jack still managed were culled. However, by then stock from this flock had been widely dispersed to the Calf of Man, and to other flocks on the island and in Britain.

Calf of Man

In 1969 Jack was asked by the museum to take a breeding group of Loghtans to the Calf of Man, a small island off the southern tip of the main island (*Plate 39*). The Calf was then owned by the National Trust for England and Wales, but leased to the Manx Museum and National Trust which became owners in 1986. The Calf had not been farmed since 1958, and it became a bird observatory in 1962. On 21st July 1969 Jack took a ram, a ewe with a lamb and two shearling ewes to the Calf (*Plate 40*); this foundation stock was photo-

39. Air photograph of the Calf from the south west with the Isle of Man behind. (Photo by Manx Technical Publications; courtesy of Malcolm Wright)

40. The historic moment on 21st July 1969 when the first Manx Museum Loghtans arrived on the Calf of Man (Photo by Lewis Barham)

graphed in part soon after its arrival by Malcolm Wright, then warden of the bird observatory (*Plates 41-2*).

A record of how the flock grew and prospered on the Calf is provided by the Bird Observatory Reports written each year by the Calf warden. They show how the numbers built up from 1969 and how they have recently been held down so that there are no more sheep than the island can support during the winter.

Year	Sheep left on the Calf at the end of each season (ewes and rams shown together unless indicated separately)
1969	4 ewes and 1 ram
1970	9
1971	7 ewes and 5 rams
1972	11 ewes and 8 rams
1973	15 ewes and 13 rams
1974	20 ewes and 20 rams
1975	34
1976	35 (10 had been removed)
1977	?
1978	65
1979	64
1980	?
1981	95
1982	62
1983	?
1984	?
1985	114
1986	121
1987	117

There is not a complete year-by-year record of the numbers of lambs reared by the number of ewes, but the details we have are interesting:

1972	7 lambs from 7 ewes
1973	10 lambs from 11 ewes
1974	12 lambs from 15 ewes
1975	22 lambs from 20 ewes

41. The ram.

42. Ewe and lamb.

1976	26 lambs from 32 ewes
1980	just over 100%
1982	63 lambs from 72 ewes

From the six years we have these precise figures, there is a total of 140 lambs from 157 ewes, that is 89% average for lambs reared in these most exposed conditions. It contrasts with 150% often recorded in lowland conditions.

The Calf flock is not truly feral because culling does take place each year and rams are sometimes removed and replaced by others from the flock kept at the north end of the island still shepherded by Jack Quine. The Calf flock has since 1975 been in the hands of Alec Maddrell (*Plate 43*) who lives nearby at Port St. Mary and was for a long time a tenant of museum land at the Cregneash folk life museum nearby.

The Calf flock is rounded up once each year in August, for clipping whatever wool is still on the sheep by then, for dipping, for worming and for the annual cull (*Plates C8-9*). The whole operation is a long and tedious process; rounding up all the sheep can itself take two days because the animals are very lively and some are almost hidden on isolated cliffs and ledges. Mature sheep are clipped and then they are all dipped to satisfy government sheep health regulations. Surplus stock are taken off the Calf by small boat; cull animals are sold in Ramsey livestock market; some ram lambs are retained for breeding and some stock is sold to other breeders.

It is possible with patience to approach the groups of sheep on the Calf and watch them graze (*Plates C6-7*). Clearly, this flock has been culled to remove most of the two-horned animals, because the flock is predominantly of four-horn type, although there are a few two-horned ewes. The rams are all four-horned. The Castlemilk influence seems stronger here than it is in the other museum flock; some of the ewes and lambs have obvious light markings around the tail, on the belly, under the chin and around the eyes. The difference between this flock managed by Alec Maddrell and the flock at the north end managed by Jack Quine demonstrates the culling preferences of the two shepherds.

To visit the Calf of Man is a real pleasure; the experience is always memorable. As someone said 'If Heaven is like the Calf I will go any day'. This small island provides the best opportunity to see the Loghtans in their natural environment, where they survive in the bleakest of conditions. They are not fed hay in winter and they have to live off the short grass, heather shoots, lichens and bulbs which they scratch up. After the annual cull in the summer, Alec Maddrell tries to leave about 100 ewes and three rams on the island for the winter. He believes that if it were not for the rabbits, which infest the island in enormous numbers, he could have a flock two to three times that size. The Calf wardens, however, are happy with the rabbits because they provide good feeding areas for choughs which eat insects which thrive in short grass. The rabbit holes make useful nesting sites for shearwaters and puffins. At times when myxamatosis reduces the rabbit population dramatically, the Loghtans are useful in keeping the grass down. Indeed, the number of nesting pairs of choughs on the island doubled during the first 10 years the sheep were on the Calf.

Boat trips run from Port Erin and Port St. Mary each day in the holiday season and by special arrangement at other times. No Loghtan enthusiast should rest until he has been to the Calf of Man.

43. Alec Maddrell, the Manx Museum's Calf shepherd with 'Bob', 1987. (Photo by Alex Maddrell)

Druidale Farm

Back at Druidale (*Plates 44-5*), the size of the Loghtan flock continued to grow during the late 1960s and surplus stock then became available. For the rare breeds enthusiast this was the first opportunity to buy Manx Loghtans, and by 1972 a 'waiting list' had accumulated at the museum in Douglas.

In the late 1960s the Curraghs Wildlife Park, between Sulby and Ballaugh, was the first on the island to establish a breeding group as an offshoot of the Manx Museum flocks (*Plate 46*). In 1970 two young ewes went to the National Agricultural Centre's flock at Stoneleigh in exchange for a young ram which was sent to the Isle of Man for the Curraghs Wildlife Park. Also in 1970 Mrs Mona Mapes at Ballaugh was the first private breeder on the island to buy sheep from the museum. The Cotswold Farm Park in Gloucestershire obtained a four-horned ram lamb in 1972 when John Neave flew one in a Cessna to Staverton airport. Joe Henson of the Cotswold Farm Park says that it caused quite a lot of interest, as Manx sheep were almost unheard of in England at that time. This ram joined a group of ewes he had obtained from the National Agricultural Centre in 1971. After these sales and the establishment of the Calf flock, numbers in the 'northern flock' were down to 47 ewes and 25 ewe lambs in December 1972.

In 1973 six ewes and a ram, the best that Jack had available, went to Stoneleigh to join their Whipsnade flock which by then consisted of 10 ewes, seven lambs and one ram (*Plate 57*). By doing this, the Manx Museum and the N.A.C. had very sensibly established a strong reserve flock outside the island to protect the breed in case of any mishaps on the island. Alastair Dymond, in charge of the Sheep Unit at the N.A.C., was quoted in the *Daily Telegraph* at the time as saying 'They are donated to us on the understanding that if anything should happen to the Manx Museum stock, they should have them back'. By 1977 he was able to say that the animals had been first class and had 'improved the Stoneleigh flock beyond recognition'.

44. Rams at Druidale in the summer of 1977. (Photo by Dennis Reed, Manx Technical Publications)

45. *Close-up of the right-hand*
Druidale ram in Plate 44.
(Photo by Dennis Reed, Manx
Technical Publications)

Sheep for sale

As it turned out, the need for a reserve flock was not so necessary because the museum was about to experience a strong demand from private breeders which would ensure that flocks would become established in the next few years in many parts of Britain.

In July 1974 the Druidale flock consisted of 12 rams, 54 ewes, 16 shearlings and 44 lambs, so the museum was able to supply the following breeders, some of whom had been waiting five years for sheep:

Mrs. P. Grant, Alvediston, Wiltshire: 1 ram and 2 ewes
Loch Lomond Bear Park, Alexandria, Dumbartonshire: 1 ram and 2 ewes (collected 1975)
Mr. I. Crowe, Isle of Man: surplus breeding ewes
Mr. L. Hindmarch, Lee Bay, Devon: 1 ram and 2 ewes
Riber Castle Wildlife Park, Matlock, Derbyshire: 2 rams and 2 ewes
Mrs B. Platt, Downholland, Lancashire: 1 ram lamb, 2 ewes and 2 ewe lambs (collected 1975)

All stock were sold for £25 each.

Gone were the dark days when 'Nobody was really that interested'. The Rare Breeds Survival Trust had been formed in 1973, and there was eager demand for these attractive horned brown sheep from the Isle of Man. The hard work during those lonely years had all been worthwhile. By the end of the year the museum flock had about 22 females less than in July, so there were probably more sales than are now recorded in Jack Quine's papers.

Demand continued to exceed supply. In response to an enquiry for sheep in January 1976, Jack wrote: 'As you say in your letter, I am pestered by people wanting to buy them and the stocks are limited. At the moment I have a waiting list of several people wanting to buy sheep and will certainly add your name to it'. Surplus stock was sold as it became available. The Manx Museum continued to give highest priority to supporting the main reserve flock at Stoneleigh, so a further six ewes and a ram went to the N.A.C. in November 1977. In addition that year, the following private breeders in Britain were also supplied with sheep:

Mr. L. Hindmarch, Lee Bay, Devon: 2 ewes
Mrs. O.M. Avery, Stockland, Devon: 2 ewes and 2 ewe lambs
Mr. C. Stewart, Isle of Coll: 3 ewes and 2 ewe lambs
Mrs A. Boraston, Anglesey: 2 2-shear ewes.

After that, demand gradually tailed off as the newly-formed breeding units on the island and in Britain themselves started to have surplus stock. Spare museum animals are now sold at Ramsey livestock market.

In 1976 the Manx Loaghtan Sheep Breed Society was formed for island breeders, and in April Jack was asked to be an Honorary Life Member and to sit on their Selectors/Judges Panel subcommittee to oversee the selection of animals for the society's breed register. Jack declined; never a committee man, he didn't feel that a society was necessary. He has, however, continued to work for the good of the breed and has gone out of his way to help individuals who come requesting advice and information. He was also luke-warm in response to the suggestion that the museum flock be registered by the Rare Breeds Survival Trust in their *Combined Flock Book*. In the end the Manx Museum flocks were not included in either the island's register or the Combined Flock Book, and they are still unregistered.

Maughold Head and The Dhoon

In 1977 Druidale Farm was sold and Jack had to leave the farm which he had managed for nearly 30 years. He took a tenancy at Grange Farm, Sulby (*Plate 37*), and the Druidale flock was moved to the Manx National Trust property at Maughold Head on the east side of the island. After the Trust had acquired land close to Dhoon Glen, a steep-sided valley overlooking the sea nearby, it was possible from 1984 onwards to alternate the flock between the two properties.

46. *A ram at the Curraghs Wildlife Park, 1977, with badly inturned upper horns and an overshot lower jaw.*
(Photo by Dennis Reed, Manx Technical Publications)

Jack still continues to manage this flock for the Manx National Trust; there are about 70 ewes and four rams which are much more accessible and tamer than the sheep on the Calf. Unlike the Calf flock, about half the 'northern' flock is made up of two-horned ewes, which undermines the myth that all Loghtan sheep on the island are four-horned. Jack sees no reason to cull out two-horned stock because he remembers quite clearly two-horned sheep in the flock well before the Soay ram was introduced in 1966. Indeed, he likes to use a two-horned ram occasionally to stop the horn pattern breaking down, with horns in the young stock coming off or growing into the face.

Cregneash and The Grove

Like all breeders, Jack has his own views about what an ideal Loghtan should be like, and each year he chooses two sets from the Dhoon flock consisting of a ram, ewe and lamb to spend the holiday season on museum properties open to the public. One set is at the remarkable Cregneash Village Folk Museum in the south end of the island where a crofting village is preserved and open to visitors (*Plate 47, C10 and back cover*). This museum is a must for anyone sight-seeing on the island; it is a most impressive example of how a living village can be conserved and used to display a way of life which disappeared between the wars.

The other set is at the Grove Museum near Ramsey. This was the family home of a Liverpool shipping merchant, and the house is displayed as a Victorian country retreat. Although the museum is advertised as a rural life museum, it hardly yet lives up that claim. Much work still needs to be done to display and interpret the farm buildings and the agricultural implements piled up in the outbuildings. Again, however, in the paddock beside the farm-house one of the Manx National Trust's breeding groups selected by Jack can easily be viewed at close quarters.

Other groups

Privately-owned groups of sheep are on view at the Tynwald Craft Centre, where clothing made of Loghtan wool is on sale, and at the Curraghs Wildlife Park.

Loghtan Sheep Sub-Committee

The Manx Museum has a sub-committee of its Trustees to administer more effective control of the Trust's flock. First formed in 1968, it meets to decide, for example, on how many animals to bring off the Calf each year and on how to utilise other Trust properties for the benefit of the flock. The committee liaises closely with the two museum shepherds who attend their meetings when necessary.

The future

Looking ahead, it is the aim of the Manx Museum to continue to maintain two flocks — the Calf flock and the 'northern' flock (Maughold Head, The Dhoon, The Grove etc.) — and as far as possible not to drop below 100 ewes and replacements in each. Breeding policy will aim at producing stock of the right type rather than select for animals suitable for the commercial exploitation of Loghtan wool.

Footnote

(1) These figures contrast with 24 breeding ewes quoted by John Olner in his 1954 BSc thesis on sheep farming practices in the Isle of Man. However, his figures are not supported by contemporary photographs (*Plates 34-6*) or by Jack Quine's memory of events. Other figures in the Olner thesis (125% for lambs reared and a lamb weight of 70-80lbs by September) also seem too high. The writer has obtained copies of some pages of the thesis, although the whole work has recently been mislaid at the University of Newcastle upon Tyne.

47. A group of Loghtans at Cregneash 1965, taken by the late Mr. Vernon Shaw while on holiday. (Photo courtesy of Mrs A.P. Shaw)

The Strathallan Flock

Nellie Keig

Meanwhile, at Strathallan, in Port St. Mary (p.38-39), Colby Cubbin and his mother had both died in 1955 leaving the house to the lady who had looked after him in his last years, Jemima Campbell. She never lived in the house and sold it to Ralf Lea in 1958 who shared it with Lord Geoffrey Percy. In 1964 Ronnie and Mary Aldrich bought the house and they have lived there ever since. Ronnie Aldrich is the well known post-war musician, who was leader of the famous Squadronaires dance band up until 1964. He is still active as a pianist and musical director for B.B.C. T.V. shows.

48. 'Stanley', a favourite ram at Strathallan 'long before the Aldriches either lived there or owned the flock' (ie pre-1964). The photograph is believed to date from about the mid 1950s. (Photo courtesy of Barbara Platt)

After the Cubbins died in 1955 the flock was looked after for the next 17 years by Nellie Keig with the help of an allowance generated from the interest on $1,000 in Ellen Cubbin's will '..for the maintenance of my animals living at Strathallan Castle Port St. Mary at my death for the period of ten years..'. Nellie Keig carried out her wishes with the support of the Port St. Mary Commissioners who probably saw some tourist potential in the animals (*Plates 48-9*). They rented her land at Queen's Road in Port St. Mary and

58

49. Another picture of Stanley in 1957 with John Guy, then aged five in 'The Paddock', now a car park in Fistard Road, Port St. Mary. To local people they were simply known as 'Nellie Keig's sheep', rather than as Loghtans. This photo provides a recorded date for the ram. (Photo courtesy of Hesba Skelly)

obtained a ram for her from the Manx Museum. This may have been the extremely bad-tempered six-horned animal which eventually died after hitting a stone wall while chasing someone who had been trying to photograph it.

The flock was also able to make use of the small fields around Strathallan Castle (*Plate 50*), for which Mary Aldrich charged Nellie Keig the rental of one fleece a year. The story of how the sheep then passed to Mary Aldrich is a touching one. On 26th January 1972 Nellie Keig sent a message to Mary asking her to visit her as quickly as possible. When Mary arrived, Nellie (who seemed in perfect health) asked if she could sign the sheep over to Mary immediately. Mary rushed home to type the following note for Nellie Keig to sign:

'TO WHOM IT MAY CONCERN
I, Nellie Keig, of Park Road, Port. St. Mary, have given my six Loughtyn sheep to Edith Mary Aldrich of Strathallan, Port. St. Mary.'

50. Barbara Platt feeding a ewe in Nellie Keig's flock at Strathallan in the mid 1950s. The picture confirms that this flock was not entirely four-horned. (Photo courtesy of Barbara Platt)

A few days later she was admitted to hospital where she died of cancer on 22 February. This episode shows the importance Nellie Keig attached to her flock and the debt we owe to her for its survival.

Mary Aldrich

The Aldriches now found themselves the owners of sheep they had never taken much notice of before. Photographs of the ram and some of the ewes at the time are preserved in the Aldrich's family album (*Plates 51-2*). Unfortunately, the flock was in a very poor state 'nothing had been done with them for years and they were literally on their last legs'. The ram very soon died of pneumonia, and Mary was then left without a ram for her first breeding season. By chance she heard of the museum flock, and was able to borrow a ram from Jack Quine for the season, an arrangement which has continued ever since in return for a ram lamb (*Plate 53*).

51. The ram at Strathallan in 1972 just after Nellie Keig passed the flock on to Mary Aldrich. It looks unwell and it died soon after this picture was taken, leaving Mary without a ram. (Photo courtesy of Mary Aldrich)

It is clear from this story that while the Strathallan stock may well have been quite separate from the museum's up until 1955, it was genetically linked to it some time after that. The figures show that the flock declined from 18 to six, presumably towards the end of Nellie Keig's custodianship. Nevertheless, it is a fact that while the museum numbers were so critically low, there were actually other animals available, even though they received no publicity and the existence of the flock was known only to a few. This is actually the only flock on the Isle of Man to survive with it own identity from the 1930s to the present day: a remarkable record.

The flock is now strong and healthy and has been maintained by the Aldriches at a level at 12 to 15 breeding ewes over the past 15 years (*Plates 55 and C11*). No detailed records have been kept of how the surplus breeding stock has been distributed, although we know a ram lamb went to the King of Swaziland in 1979 (*Plate 54*), two ewes went to Ivor Crowe at Ballaugh and a ram lamb and three ewes went to Luke Hindmarch in Devon both in the early 1970s. Stock from this flock must by now be well distributed both on the

*52. Ewes and lambs in the
Strathallan flock in 1972.
(Photo courtesy of Mary Aldrich)*

island and in Britain. The importance of the genetic contribution which this flock has made to the present overall breeding population is discussed later (p.100).

Footnote

The two last chapters have been written with much assistance from Jack Quine, who has provided access to his own papers which cover the period from 1966 to the present, from Mary Aldrich, who has given the writer all the information she has on the Strathallan flock. Larch Garrad of the Manx Museum has patiently answered specific questions about the museum flock as far as her memory and other museum pressures will allow. Unfortunately, however, it has *not* been possible to read the Manx Museum's letter files and other papers on the management of the museum flock. If these are ever opened to researchers, some details may need to be modified and, no doubt, additional information will become available.

*53. A fine photograph of a ram
on loan from Jack Quine at
Strathallan in 1981 or 1982.
(Photo courtesy of Mary Aldrich)*

54. In 1979 the British Foreign Office arranged the export of a ram lamb from the Strathallan flock and shearling ewe from the museum's northern flock to go to the King of Swaziland. There has been no news back yet on whether there is now a flock of Loghtans in Swaziland. (Photo courtesy of Mary Aldrich)

55. Mary Aldrich with her flock at Strathallan in 1988. (Photo by Peter Wade-Martins)

The Rare Breeds Survival Trust
(1973-1989)

The story becomes better documented

This book is primarily concerned with the history of the Manx Loghtan on the Isle of Man and how it survived the years when it was most in danger. However, the story would not be complete without a description of how the Loghtans became popular amongst rare breeds enthusiasts all over Britain through the work of the Rare Breeds Survival Trust.

With so many people and so many flocks entwined within the saga, it is no simple task to identify the most significant moments. One reason for this may be that we are too close to see events with an historic perspective. Nevertheless, we must try, and the task is made easier by the fact that, unlike the Isle of Man, developments in Britain are very well documented.

There is the glossy magazine called *The Ark* which has been published by the Trust every month since May 1974. There is also the *Combined Flock Book* produced annually since 1975. This *Flock Book* was actually established in 1974 as a private venture between Michael Rosenberg, who later became the Trust's Honorary Director and President, and Lawrence Alderson, the Trust's Technical Consultant. It was published by Countrywide Livestock Ltd. from Lawrence Alderson's office in Haltwistle, Northumberland until it was handed over to the Trust as a going concern in 1980. The *Flock Book* provides a very detailed pedigree of every animal entered.

The catalogue of the Show and Sale held each September at the National Agricultural Centre at Stoneleigh is itself an important record of the breeders and the sheep they were offering for sale. Fortunately, the auctioneer's records are preserved, and they will be available for future study. Finally, there is the Trust's annual surveys of flocks carried out by sending a questionnaire or 'Flock Return' to all breeders asking them to identify numbers of animals and the details of their breeding programmes.

This chapter will only be a summary of events; those wishing to pursue details further can easily consult the records listed above. The only aspect which is not well documented is the story of how the Manx Loghtan arrived in mainland Britain to form the foundation stock for the present breeding population as listed in the 1974 *Flock Book*.

The Loghtans arrive in Britain

(Note: Sheep registration numbers shown in brackets in this section are those listed in the *Combined Flock Book*)

Unlike the Hebridean sheep, which were well established as a park sheep in Britain in the nineteenth century, the Manx Loghtan did not gain a foothold until 1955, when the first group arrived at London Zoo (p.47). Their descendants were then transferred to the National Agricultural Centre at Stoneleigh in 1968, to be supplemented by further imports from the Isle of Man in the 1970s (p.53 & 55).

Enquiries have revealed that the next group to arrive were imported in

about 1964 by Riber Castle Wildlife Park near Matlock in Derbyshire. Eddie Hallam, then Director of the Park, obtained them with the help of Douglas Kerruish, the Manx government veterinary officer. Details of which flock they were from are no longer available, but the remnants of this stock are probably those ewes described in the 1975 *Flock Book* as bred by 'IOM Min of Agr' (919-920). Riber Castle enlarged their flock with more from the Manx Museum in 1974 (917-918) (p.55). Eddie Hallam, now retired from the Park, remembers that in the 1960s, when rare breeds were not yet fashionable, there was very little interest in the sheep.

However, when the newly formed Cotswold Farm Park in Gloucestershire flew in a young ram from the island in 1972 all that had changed; because of the fresh groundswell of interest in minority breeds the strange four-horned ram caused much excitement (p.53). Unfortunately he later died of pasturella pneumonia without leaving progeny. The foundation stock at the Cotswold Farm Park started in 1970 with a Whipsnade ram (876) sold to the Farm Park by the National Agricultural Centre at Stoneleigh because he was attacking everything and everybody in sight, including stockmen. As the Farm Park then had no other Manx sheep, they put him with some Jacob and Hill Radnor ewes in the first year. In 1971 they had the use of some ewes from Stoneleigh bought by Mrs Mona Mapes; the two parties then shared the progeny. In 1973 Stoneleigh sold the Cotswold Farm Park some ewes (883-6), and the stock built up from there.

So, to begin with there were three breeding groups in England: at Stoneleigh, at Riber Castle and at the Cotswold Farm Park. This list was very quickly supplemented by the activities of other enthusiasts. Major Armstrong-Wilson in Cumbria obtained a ram (fathered by 876) from the Cotswold Farm Park in about 1973 (805) which he used on a group of four ewes he bought from the Curraghs Wildlife Park on the Isle of Man the following year (807-810). Peter Furness in Derbyshire started a flock with some elderly sheep (a ram and two ewes) he bought from Riber Castle in 1972 or 1973. In 1974, Riber Castle, the Grants in Wiltshire and Luke Hindmarch in Devon all imported Manx Museum Loghtans. The Grants were adding to

stock they had from Stoneleigh (821-823 & 825), while Luke Hindmarch was supplementing stock he had obtained from the Curraghs Wildlife Park (872 & 874), the Cotswold Farm Park (873) and Stoneleigh (875). The next year Barbara Platt in Lancashire obtained Manx Museum stock (914-5 & L0038-9) to add to a ram lamb she had from Stoneleigh in 1973 (804) and three ewes she had from Stoneleigh in 1974 (835-837); two of these were elderly Whipsnade animals. Other breeders quickly bought stock from the original three flocks, although in the autumn of 1975 Ken Briggs from Worcestershire went around the Isle of Man collecting unwanted sheep. He picked up a ram from the Kneale brothers at Ballacaley (921) and six ewes (922-7) and two lambs (L0045-6) from Lt. Col. Spittall of Injebreck who had only shortly before obtained them from the Curraghs Wildlife Park. Later, Luke Hindmarch seems to have bought two ewes from Mary Aldrich in 1977 when he collected further stock from the Manx Museum. No other sheep from her Strathallan flock are shown in the *Flock Books*, but indirectly the influence of this flock on the British population must be considerable (p.99).

By the time registrations for the first *Combined Flock Book* closed at the end of 1974, 15 breeders had registered 63 pure-bred females; from there on numbers steadily increased (**Table 1**)[1].

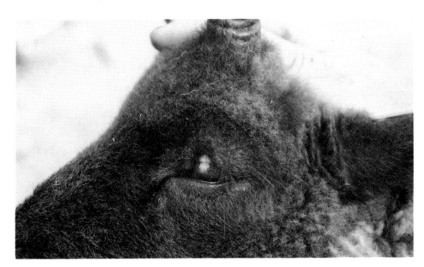

58. A Loghtan lamb with split eyelid. (Photo by Edward Wade-Martins)

Although breeders experimented with cross breeding, using primarily Jacobs and Soays, it seems from the *Flock Book* that these crosses have contributed very little to the present British Manx Loghtan population; they were quickly weeded out as numbers increased.

The Ark

The first issue of *The Ark* appeared in May 1974, one year after the foundation of the Trust, and this announced arrangements for the registration programme. The next and subsequent issues carried advertisements for cattle and sheep breeders saying: 'Register your animals now'. The result of this campaign was *The Combined Flock Book* Vol. 1 (1975) for animals registered in 1974; for Loghtans this included stock imported from the Isle of Man and others descended from animals bred in Britain over the previous twenty years.

59-64. The next six scenes, taken in 1988, show the sequence of events at the most popular of Rare Breeds events in Britain: the Show and Sale organised each year at the National Agricultural Centre at Stoneleigh.

In May 1975 the results of the first registration programme was reviewed as follows:

59. Sheep are first conducted, using various means, to the pens after the veterinary inspection. (Photo by Peter Wade-Martins)

The Manx Loghtan is one of the three breeds having a population of less than 200 breeding ewes, according to the 1974 Survey. Volume I of the Flock Book lists only sixty five 'pure' females, placing it one behind the Portland with an entry of sixty-six. It is believed that all of the major flocks in England are included in the Programme. There are, however, several flocks on the Isle of Man which are as yet unregistered. The population of these is thought to be somewhat greater in total than the English flocks, and there is also a small feral population on the Isle of Man.

There are presently fourteen registered flocks, and their size varies greatly, the three largest accounting for forty two of the female entries. As of December

31st (1974) three of the other flocks were comprised of 'grade' females, leaving the remaining twenty-three divided between eight owners. We are advised that participants in the Programme have been able to import a total of approximately twelve females since 1st January and while their arrival was too late for inclusion in Volume I, it is hoped that they, and their 1975 progeny, will be included in Volume II.[2]

Because of the extremely limited amount of 'pure' stock, several Manx Loghtan breeders have embarked upon 'grading-up' schemes, which account for a further thirteen entries. So far all of these are based on a Manx Loghtan Jacob cross. The type of progeny from the first, and succeeding crosses, has been varied, and one breeder has reported the birth of an almost pure white lamb this season. While not directly relevant to the Registration Programme, it is interesting to note that some of the first cross females have attained growth in excess of either of their parent breeds.

This led to some correspondence in *The Ark* starting in November 1975 with a fairly strong letter from Ivor Crowe, the founder of the Isle of Man's breed society. He was deeply critical of the way the Loghtans in Britain were being graded-up from cross-bred stock, with lambs which were the daughters of first cross ewes being entered in the *Combined Flock Book*. Then began a long and rather tense period in relations between the Trust and the island's

60. Once in the pens, the sheep are numbered and prospective buyers have a chance to view the choice available at close quarters. (Photo by Peter Wade-Martins)

society; there remained a frostiness which was not fully thawed until the Manx Loghtan Sheep Breeders Group visited the island in May 1988. The differences of view had ranged over issues like cross breeding, the number of horns which are true-to-type and the prevalence of split eyelids. As a result of all this, the island breeders did not join the registration programme offered through the *Combined Flock Book*.

In September 1975 Luke Hindmarch's flock in Devon, one of the earliest to be established in Britain, was featured. This article mentioned the exhaustive survey he had just completed of almost every Loghtan in Britain during which he had photographed the animals and studied inheritance of characteristics in detail. This record could be a most useful source of information in years to come, but 15 years later, his notes and photographic catalogue are still in his

own particular shorthand, not decipherable by anyone else. Let us hope that he will soon find time in his busy life to remedy this situation.

The first picture of a Loghtan to appear in *The Ark* was a four-horned ram, with a white patch between the horns, with white socks and a white tail (*Plate 56*). This was in the September 1974 issue as part of a description of rare breeds at Acton Scott Hall.

In January 1975, the National Agricultural Centre's own Manx flock was featured with a picture showing both two-horned and four-horned ewes (*Plate 57*). This was accompanied by the following short piece:

> The flock of Manx Loghtans have been virtually reconstituted in the last few years. The N.A.C. is now working in co-operation with the Manx Museum and National Trust and using the latter organisation's standards as a guideline. These call for four 'curly' horns, and an absence of any white markings. While regretting the lack of proven history of this breed, Mr. Dymond considers that it has considerable potential because of its hardiness, and he was pleasantly surprised by the results of an accidental visit paid by the Manx Loghtan ram to the Stoneleigh commercial flock. When the breed is on a healthier footing, he thinks it may have a value for crossing purposes.

While it is not necessary to list every article or letter which subsequently appeared in *The Ark*, mention should be drawn to Libby Henson's report, in the April 1981 issue, of her survey of the prevalence of split eyelids in Loghtans in the Isle of Man. Split eyelid is a condition where a notch or a v-shaped indent in the upper eyelid disfigures the eye (*Plate 58*), but apparently does little to effect the health of the animal. It is probably linked to the gene which determines that an animal will have four horns rather than two, and it is most common in flocks made up largely of four-horned stock. The results showed that split eyelid were to be found on island flocks, despite claims to the contrary; this defect seems to have no detrimental effect on the animal's ability to survive even in the most exposed conditions.

Flock trends

The best way to follow the spread of Loghtan flocks throughout Britain after the original ones were established in the early 1970s is to examine the figures derived from the registrations in the *Combined Flock Book*. **Table 1**, based on

62. Here Dr. Richard Harper-Smith, the judge of the primitive breeds, is taking a close look at Mrs Boraston's ram which he eventually selected as breed champion (Plate 69). (Photo by Simon Tupper)

computer print-outs provided by the R.B.S.T., sets out the number of recorded females according to year of birth, the number of breeders registering stock each year and the average number of females registered by breeders. Just a few animals were already elderly when registration began in 1974.

Table 1: Registration of females by year of birth

Year of Birth	No. of females (incl. grade and provisional)	No. of breeders	Av. No. females registered per breeder
Not recorded	100		
1962	2		
1965	2		
1969	3		
1970	7		
1971	29		
1972	17		
1973	25		
1974	55	15	3.6
1975	56	18	3.1
1976	72	12	6.0
1977	88	18	4.8
1978	82	19	4.3
1979	125	22	5.7
1980	158	27	5.8
1981	189	31	6.1
1982	196	38	5.1
1983	270	50	5.4
1984	270	56	4.8
1985	236	51	4.6
1986	208	53	3.9
1987	229	60	3.8
1988	280	69	4.1
TOTAL	2,699		

The most encouraging aspect of this table is the steady increase in the number of breeders from 15 in 1974 to 69 in 1988. Registrations, however, reached a peak in 1983/4 and then fell back until 1988.

The distribution of breeders registering pure-bred stock in 1987 is shown in **Fig. 2**. It can be seen from this that they are predominantly clustered in the south of England and the Midlands, hardly the environment in which the Loghtans are designed to provide the best returns from poor grazing. This pattern underlines the impression given in **Table 1** that it is still currently a fancier's sheep. With small flock sizes and a largely lowland distribution, the breed has a long way to go before it can in any way be said to be demonstrating its commercial potential. Still, the mere fact that there are 60 or so registered flocks, plus an unknown number of others, is a remarkable change from the 1960s when that same map would be completely blank except for one dot over Whipsnade Zoo and another over Riber Castle.

The main mechanism by which stock has been distributed to new breeders is the annual Show and Sale organised by the R.B.S.T. at the National Agricultural Centre at Stoneleigh (*Plates 59-70*). The numbers offered for sale and the average prices of females provide an interesting insight into the relationship between supply and demand for a breed of livestock not fashionable amongst commercial farmers; in this situation the numbers produced can easily be greater than the market can absorb.

Table 2: R.B.S.T. Show and Sale prices for females and numbers forward (shown in brackets) for sale 1975-1988

1975	ewes £45 (*c*.4)	average £45 (*c*.4)
1976	(not available)	average £52.50 (7)
1977	ewes £44.35 (22)	
	lambs £65.10 (6)	average £47.25 (28)
1978	ewes £47.00 (33)	
	lambs £64.00 (16)	average £47.54 (49)
1979	ewes £59.03 (27)	
	lambs £57.99 (20)	average £58.59 (47)
1980	ewes £19.95 (46)	
	lambs £28.27 (18)	average £22.29 (64)
1981	ewes £40.29 (45)	
	lambs £28.47 (21)	average £36.53 (66)
1982	ewes £28.30 (21)	
	lambs £36.25) (19)	average £32.08 (40)
1983	ewes £30.35 (11)	
	lambs £16.51 (29)	average £20.31 (40)
1984	ewes £41.58 (33)	
	lambs £19.59 (35)	average £30.26 (68)
1985	ewes £24.34 (44)	
	lambs £20.48 (38)	average £22.55 (82)
1986	ewes £43.16 (18)	
	lambs £51.98 (10)	average £46.31 (28)
1987	ewes £55.65 (10)	
	lambs £45.51 (23)	average £48.58 (33)
1988	ewes £63.00 (22)	average £58.52 (37)
	lambs £51.94 (15)	
1989	ewes £108.06 (12)	average £80.07 (40)
	lambs £79.50 (28)	

Prices started fairly high with so few animals available, and they reached a peak of £58.59 in 1979, with 47 entries. Then, as numbers rose still further and supply exceeded demand, the prices collapsed the next year to £22.29, under half the previous year's average. In response to this, entries dropped in the

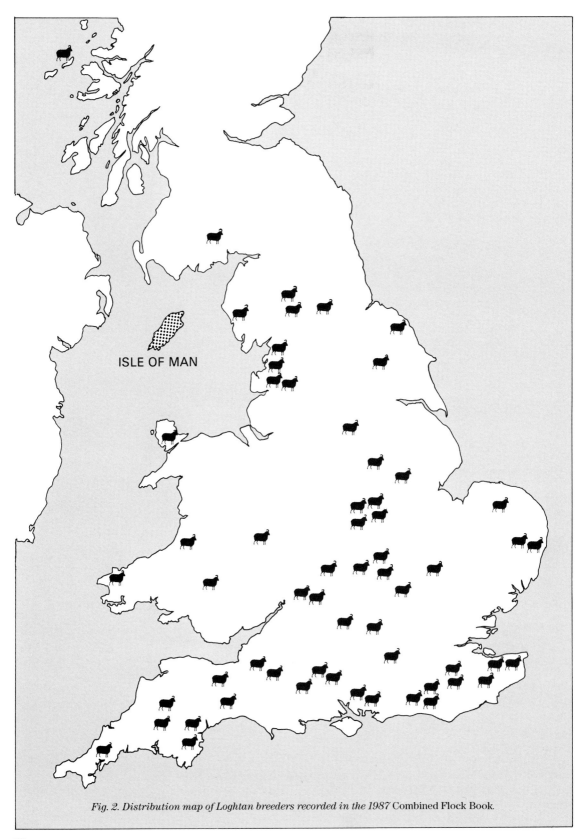

ISLE OF MAN

Fig. 2. Distribution map of Loghtan breeders recorded in the 1987 Combined Flock Book.

63. The ewe (L2295) which won first prize in the ewe class in 1988; the white spectacles are a feature of the Castlemilk influence (contrast with C13); such light markings should not be confused with the completely white patches as seen in Plates 56 and C15. (Photo by Peter Wade-Martins)

two succeeding years and then rose again to a new peak in 1985 when again prices fell. It appears that a pattern is emerging, with the numbers forward for sale reflecting optimism or pessimism based on the previous year's results. In turn, prices then respond to numbers available. It will be interesting to see whether this cyclical pattern is repeated in the years ahead or whether better promotion by the Breeders Group will establish long-term price stability.

Table 3: Analysis of Flock Returns for 1984 — 1987

	1984	1985	1986	1987
No. of breeders registering stock	57	50	53	60
No. of flock returns received	48	45	42	49
No. of ewes	434	417	378	350
No. of ewe lambs born in year	209	196	165	187
No. of rams	43	37	38	36
No. of ram lambs retained	37	23	34	31
No. of lambs born in year	472	538	418	500
Total no. of sheep (excluding whethers)	723	640	561	503
No. of ewes being mated pure	426	352	270	286
No. of ewes being cross-bred	48	88	106	89
Flock averages.	15	14	13 (1-51)	9 (females)

The remarkable upturn in 1989 was surprising at a time when prices for commercial sheep were down and there was a general shortage of grass caused by dry weather.

Following the years of over supply, breeders have experimented with cross breeding to reduce their output of pure-bred stock and to find new ways of breeding from their Loghtans profitably. The average number of pure-bred lambs registered per breeder (**Table 1**) fell gradually but consistently since reaching a high point in the period 1979/1981, reflecting the trend towards cross breeding. This, of course, is an alternative outlet for lambs from poorer quality ewes.

Flock Returns

Since 1982 the Trust has asked breeders to complete a Flock Return showing their breeding plans for the coming year. Although the results do not survive for the first two years and not all breeders complete the form, the returns for 1984-1987 are enough to demonstrate general trends (**Table 3**). What they don't, of course, show is how people who have bought Loghtans just for cross breeding are using them, because these shepherds tend to disappear from sight and there is no feed-back on their activities.

The steady increase in the number of ewes being used for crossing up to 1986 was reversed in 1987, probably in response to the improvement in value of pure-bred stock at the 1986 Show and Sale.

Island Heritage woollen products

While many breeders either use their Loghtan wool themselves or sell it to local hand spinners, 'Island Heritage' run by Sheelagh and Jack Holmes in Lancashire, has offered breeders an opportunity to pool all their wool so that it can be converted into lengths of tweed or knitting wool which breeders can have back to sell or use themselves. In addition, fleeces are purchased from

65. The breed champion and interbreed champion at the 1984 Show and Sale; this is Mrs Boraston's famous ewe 'Garianane Felicity' (L1103) which fetched a record price of £550 guineas, sold to Michael Rosenberg at Ash Farm, Devon. (Photo by Simon Tupper)

66. The 1985 Show and Sale breed champion: Mary Steele's ram 'Lindfield Ginger' (L1796). (Photo by Simon Tupper)

breeders and made up into a variety of skirts, jackets, hats and knitware which Sheelagh then sells at agricultural shows and other appropriate events (*Plates 71 and C18*). The business started in 1981 in a small way, but was only able to expand when the Wool Marketing Board relaxed its regulations and allowed her to buy larger quantities of fleeces direct from breeders (about 150 fleeces in 1986). Besides Loghtan fleeces, she also handles North Ronaldsay and Hebridean wool which produce pale grey and black tweeds respectively. The fleece is processed at commercial woollen mills where about 50% is lost partly because of the relatively small quantities involved and partly because of the shorter staple of the Loghtan fleece.

Sheelagh's view is that there is no reason why sales of processed Loghtan wool should not continue to increase over the next few years. However, as

67. The 1986 Show and Sale breed champion: W.H. McAlpine's four-horned ewe lamb (L2364). (Photo by Simon Tupper)

68. The 1987 Show and Sale breed champion: Cotswold Farm Park's 'Bemborough Gracious' (L2499). (Photo by Simon Tupper)

she points out, apart from the unique moorit colour, its biggest attraction for the customer is that the sheep is a rare breed. Once Loghtans move out of this category, sales will depend on marketing, on the quality of the wool and on other commercial pressures. As the fleece numbers increase, market forces are likely to reduce prices for the breeder and produce a surplus of poorer fleeces, as indeed Jacob breeders have found.

In 1988 Tynwald Mills on the Isle of Man also started to buy Loghtan wool from British flocks at very attractive prices, so it seems that it will be some time before Loghtan breeders find themselves producing more wool than the market can absorb.

69. The 1988 Show and Sale breed champion: Mrs Boraston's 'Garianane Johnny Boy' (L2572). (Photo by Simon Tupper)

70. The 1989 Show and Sale breed champion: the author's 'Longhouse Ivor' (L3320). (Photo by Simon Tupper)

Commercial evaluation trials
(Based on information supplied by Lawrence Alderson)

The R.B.S.T. has recently started to record accurately the results of crossbreeding Loghtans using commercial sires. The trials are still at an early stage and on a small scale, but preliminary results are most promising. The ewes, because of their small size, can be used most effectively to produce quality lamb.

It is efficient to mate relatively small ewes to larger terminal sires (*Plates 72-74*). This combines the advantages of a high stocking rate with low ewe maintenance costs and a high value output. A flock of 153 Manx Loghtan ewes

71. Sheelagh and Jack Holmes with their hats and other Loghtan wool products on sale at their Island Heritage stand during the 1988 Show and Sale. (Photo by Simon Tupper)

(40 kg liveweight) can be maintained on the same feed input as 100 Mule ewes (73.75 kg liveweight). When both are mated to a terminal ram (Suffolk, Charollais, Hampshire Down and Dorset Down rams have been used in the trials) the Loghtan ewes will produce 13-14% more carcass weight of lamb per acre than the Mules.

In Lowland conditions Loghtan ewes rear on average a lamb crop of 155% (compared with 175% for Mules) and the crossbred lambs are then slaughtered off grass at about 15.5 kg (compared with 18.5 kg for Mules). Results have shown that the Loghtan has similar characteristics to the Hebridean, being long-lived and milky, and is superior to the Shetland in these respects.

Early Lambing

Recent experiments on a small flock at a Coventry school, where the Loghtan ewes are induced to lamb in January, using hormone-impregnated vaginal

Table 4: 1988 results of a small early lambing flock producing Charollais and Suffolk cross Loghtans at Coventry Preparatory School.

Birth weight (kg)		4.00
6 week weight (kg)		13.37
dlg. birth — 6 weeks (g/day)		223
Slaughter Liveweight (kg)		35.11
carcass wt. (kg)		17.54
killing out %	49.9	
Days to slaughter		105
dlg. 6 weeks to slaughter (g/day)		343

sponges. has shown some encouraging growth rates with creep feed. The results are set out in **Table 4**. When Loghtan ewes are crossed with terminal sires they can produce early lambs with the size and finish comparable with cross-bred lambs from other ewes currently in commercial use.

So, whether it is for intensive early lamb production or for later lambs fed off grass, where stocking rates are the important factor, the Loghtan could have an important role to play in the modern farming industry. It just needs to be given a chance to demonstrate its potential on a commercial scale where the numbers are large enough to be statistically valid.

72. Experiments with cross breeding have produced some remarkably consistent results. The lambs always have the appearance of the sire and will soon outgrow their mothers, as this pair of young Shropshire-cross lambs demonstrated at the 1987 Loghtan Breeders Workshop. (Photo by Mike Naughton; courtesy of the Rare Breeds Survival Trust)

73. Fast-growing Charollais-cross lambs with their mother at the 1987 Breeder's Workshop. (Photo by Mike Naughton; courtesy of the Rare Breeds Survival Trust)

74. *A pair of four-month old Suffolk-cross lambs with their Loghtan mother at the author's farm at North Elmham, 1988. At this age Suffolk-cross lambs are almost as big as their mother. (Photo by Peter Wade-Martins)*

Footnotes

(1) The *Combined Flock Book* breed description, as used by the Rare Breeds Survival Trust reads as follows:

The Manx Loghtan is a small sheep which is related to the short-tailed breeds of Northern Europe. Mature ewes weigh about 38.5kg (85lbs). The animals are fine-boned and late maturing. In some cases the withers are prominent, but more usually the hind-quarters are the highest part of the back. The tail is not long enough to reach the hocks.

The wool is dark brown in colour, but becomes paler where it is exposed to bleaching agents such as the sun. The wool is soft and demi-lustre, with a staple length of 8-12 cms (3-5 ins). The Bradford Count is 44-48.

The face and legs are rich brown colour. White markings appearing on any part of the body disqualify the sheep from registration. The nose is straight and the head is of medium size. Generally both sexes have two or more horns, often four. Polled ewes occasionally occur but are undesirable. The horns of the ewes are small, while those of the rams are strong and large, but they should not grow into the face or head, nor should they impede grazing.

(In earlier versions white markings were just described as 'undesirable', but they became a disqualifying feature in the 1987 edition; this sequence is explained in detail by Alastair Dymond in a useful letter to *The Ark* for October 1988, p. 367-8.)

(2) A 'grade' animal is a crossbred; in 'grading-up' the influence of the other breed is gradually reduced in successive generations.

The Manx Loaghtan
Sheep Breed Society
(1976-1989)

The revival of Loghtans in the Isle of Man

How interest in the breed has fluctuated in the island in modern times is best revealed by a study of the entries for the islands two agricultural shows. No complete sets of show catalogues for the Royal Manx Agricultural Society or the Southern Agricultural Society are known to survive, but a fairly comprehensive collection covering the 1930s and the period from the 1950s to the present day is in the possession of Harvey Briggs, agricultural correspondent of *The Isle of Man Examiner*. He has collated the evidence for Loghtan entries from these catalogues, and the results, when combined with information in contemporary issues of the *Isle of Man Weekly Times*, are as follows.

For the 1920s and 1930s, there is no mention of Loghtans at the Royal (then the Isle of Man) Agricultural Show at all. Indeed, we know from the *Isle of Man Weekly Times* that classes suitable for Loghtans had died out by 1920 (p.16). For the Southern Agricultural Show there were no classes for Loghtans until 1924. Then, in an attempt to revive interest in the breed, Mrs Moore of Great Meadow (or Mrs Riggall as she later became) presented a set of three silver flower vases for the best pen of Manx sheep (*Plate 75*). There were prize winners in this class for exhibitors of pens of 'one Manx ram and two Manx sheep' (presumably ewes) over the next 11 years as follows:

1924	1st and 2nd J.T. Quirk, Ballacosnahan
1925	1st and 2nd J. Quirk, Ballacosnahan, Patrick
	3rd Mrs Moore, Great Meadow
1926	1st Mrs Moore, Great Meadow
	2nd J.T. Quirk, Ballacosnahan, St. John's
1927	1st J.S. Cubbon, Castletown
	2nd J.T. Gell, Castletown
	3rd C. Faragher, Castletown
1928	No entries
1929	1st Gordon Cubbon, Castletown
1930	1st Gordon Cubbon, Castletown
1931	No entries
1932	1st R. Quirk, Junr.
	2nd H. Cobbon & Son
1933	1st R. Quirk
1934	1st John Quirk, jnr, Langness, Malew.

We know that J.T. Quirk at Ballacosnahan and Mrs Moore bought stock from Bacon's flock (p.28 & 30), but the succeeding names are shadowy figures.

For 1932 there were two entries, from Henry Cubbon of Castletown and Reggie Quirk of Ballaquaggin, Malew (*Plate 76*), not far from Seafield. In 1933 there was just one entry, from Reggie Quirk. His widow, Mrs Isa Quirk, remembers that in that year he won the flower vases outright.

Finally, the newspaper records a prizewinner for 1934, although the entry is not shown in the catalogue. This was a significant year, because it was the last

75. The three solid silver flower vases competed for at the Isle of Man Southern Agricultural Show from 1924 to 1933. On the larger vase are the words:

'Isle of Man Southern District Agricultural Society, presented by Mrs G. Moore, Great Meadow, for pen of Manx sheep. Won by

1924 Mr. J.T. Quirk

1925 Mr. J.T. Quirk'

After 1925 the winner's names were not inscribed. In 1933 Reggie Quirk was the last to win them, and they are still in the possession of his widow, Mrs Isa Quirk. (Photo courtesy of Mrs. Isa Quirk)

time that Loghtans competed at an agricultural show as commercial sheep. The *Isle of Man Weekly Times* usually ignored Loghtans in its commentaries on the shows, but in that year it included the following piece, almost as a farewell to the breed.

> Considerable interest was taken by visitors in a pen of three Manx four-horned sheep, shown by Mr. R. Quirk of Langness, a breed which has almost died out. They were at one time much prized for the delicate flavour of their flesh and the fine quality of their wool, which has the added virtue that it can be woven into cloth without being dyed. The sheep were called 'Loaghtan', on account of the brown colour of the cloth made from their wool. In the days when the common lands were free for grazing most crofters owned a few Loaghtans, as they are handy and can live on almost nothing, but except at Langness and in some of the wild land of Dalby there are now none to be seen.

Thereafter, interest dwindled, and the breed came very close to extinction, as we have seen in previous chapters.

The first sign of renewed enthusiasm at the Royal Manx Show was evident in 1953 when a class was organised for three 'Manx Loughtyn' females, but there were no entries. Then, in 1954 this same class had two entries from 'Drummond and Brownsdon, Michael', presumably with sheep from Druidale Farm (p.44). In 1955 there were four entries, two from 'Drummond and Brownsdon' and two from Stanley Wood of Peel. For 1956 there were two entries, again from 'Drummond and Brownsdon'. For 1958 and 1959 there was only on entry each time, from H. Creer of Braddan. Then, throughout the 1960s there was a succession of years when the class was retained, but there were no entries, except once, from Capt. Drummond in 1962. Interest was clearly still at a very low ebb.

A real revival did not start until 1977 when Ivor Crowe of Ballaugh had four pens in one class of two males and/or females of 'Loaghtan' sheep. Today there are six classes; in 1986, for example, these were filled with 35 entries comprising 47 sheep.

For the Southern District Show the story of the revival is much the same: it all happened quickly in the late 1970s. There were four classes for 'Loughtyn sheep — Manx' for the first time in 1973, but no entries. In 1974 there was one entry in each class from Mary Aldrich. For 1975 there were no entries. From

76. Reggie Quirk of Ballaquaggin with his rams, 24 September 1929. (Photo courtesy of Mrs Isa Quirk)

1976 to 1978 there was one entry in each class from Ivor Crowe. Thereafter interest increased as the island's breed society became established. The success of the society owes much to Ivor Crowe's interest and enthusiasm for the breed.

Formation of the Society

The Manx Loaghtan Sheep Breed Society was founded in April 1976, and nearly 30 people joined at the inaugural meeting. Their aims were to form a gathering point for all those on the island with an interest in the future of the breed, to set a standard for the breed and to create a register for those animals which conformed to the standard. The president was, and still is, Mr. (now Sir) Charles Kerruish, Speaker of the House of Keys (the island's parliament), who was also on the museum's own Loghtan Sheep Subcommittee. The chairman was Ivor Crowe, who had been a founder member of the Rare Breeds Survival Trust. The secretary was Mrs Mona Mapes, the first person to establish a private flock as an offshoot of the museum flock in 1970.

The Society decided to write its own breed standard, rather than use the one already established by the Rare Breeds Survival Trust. Likewise, rather than encourage members to join R.B.S.T.'s *Combined Flock Book*, the decision was taken to create a separate Breed Register. In a newspaper report of the Society's first A.G.M. in 1977, again in the Bowling Green Hotel in Douglas, the chairman is quoted as saying that there would be two breed registers: an 'A' register for the highest quality sheep showing the best breed characteristics, and a 'B' register for sheep which in succeeding generations could be graded up to 'A' standard. The register would cover Loghtan sheep everywhere, not only in the Isle of Man, and inspectors would travel to flocks to assess their true breed merit. The Society had drawn up a 16-point list of breed characteristics — the first time this had been done in the long history of the breed[1].

The list of these breed characteristics is appended as a footnote at the end of this chapter (p.88-89); readers will see that all sheep have to be four-horned to qualify for the register, while the R.B.S.T. has accepted that a Loghtan can just as well have two horns. The Society's insistence that Loghtans need be four-horned was emphasised again in their booklet *The Manx Loaghtan Sheep: the breed that refused to die*, published in 1984.

77. Keith Shimmin with the Supreme Champion at the Manx Loaghtan Sheep Breed Society's 1987 Show. (Photo by John Maddrell)

Loaghtan Sheep Fair

The high point in the Society's year is the Loaghtan Sheep Fair held on 5th July, old St.John's Eve, the island's National Day. The Society is rightly proud of what it has achieved in establishing this event as a significant one in the island's calendar. It has been held at various locations, including Ballaugh and Great Meadow. The 1987 event, held at St. John's, close to Tynwald Hill, the old Manx parliament's meeting place, was described by Fenella Bazin, the daughter of Ivor Crowe and currently the Society's press officer, in an article in *The Ark* for April 1988 as follows:

> For the first time, the show was held over a full day, with a continuous programme of supporting events. Falconry displays, a band, traditional Manx dancers, whose costume is based on Loaghtan cloth, and traditional Manx music played by the children of St. John's Junior School.

> Beside the 50 sheep vying for the championship, there were exhibitions of spinning, competitions for the best spun wool, and finished garments, a demonstration of traditional Manx country crafts, and an exhibition outlining the story of the Loaghtan sheep. A steady stream of visitors began well before the official opening time, and continued right through the day, watching the judging, the spinning, and talking to the exhibitors. They ranged from children who had never actually touched a sheep before, to farmers and shepherds with a lifetime's experience.

> Our judge was Mr Jack Quine, well known to the RBST at Stoneleigh. The supreme champion was entered by Keith Shimmin, with Reserve and Best-Opposite-Sex owned by Mr Keith Corlett. Aaron Curphey won the trophy for the best Junior Handler, succeeding his brother Stephen, last year's winner, who was away at the Royal Show at Stoneleigh helping to show cattle.

In 1987 the 50 sheep entries were competing in eight classes for cups and rosettes (*Plate 77*), although entries were down to 31 in 1988. There were also 11 classes for handicraft entries with a Loghtan theme, including hand spinning, hand weaving, knitting and crochet (*Plate 78*).

Cross breeding

While primarily concerned with preserving and promoting the breed, the society is well aware of the Loghtan's potential as a producer of cross-bred lamb:

In the last two or three years the future of the breed has seemed much more secure, and this aim will continue to be the priority of the Society. However, some cross-breeding has been happening, both planned and accidental! This has been recognised by the Society with the introduction in 1986 of a special class, which has included cross-bred Cheviots, Blue Leicester, Suffolk, Black Welsh and Texels. Results have been interesting. The meat has been grading extremely well, especially in the early lambs. As a rule, the natural resistance of the Loaghtan to foot-rot, fly-strike and other problems is transferred to the cross-bred animals, which tend to retain the appearance of the non-Loaghtan parent. Incidentally, all the Loaghtans at the Show were four-horned, and none showed signs of split eyelids.

Perhaps the most outstanding achievement yet by a Loaghtan cross was at the Annual Manx Christmas Fatstock Show in 1986. Second only to a pen of Texel lambs was a pair of Loaghtan x Dorset Horn ewes owned by Sir Charles Kerruish. In the opinion of UK butcher Mr Chris Coomer, these were better than 21 entries of so-called improved breeds.

The island's registration programme

The Society has, however, been less successful with its registration programme. At the 1981 A.G.M. the chairman was still urging members to have their flocks registered, but it seems that many never were. Each animal was supposed to be carefully inspected, and then a tattoo punched in the ears showing flock number and the number of the individual animal. However, records have not been kept up-to-date, and no animal has been inspected or registered for the last five years; it seems that the recording system has broken down. In response to this situation and the warm welcome and kindness the society showed to British breeders during their visit to the island in May 1988, the R.B.S.T. followed that event by immediately offering free registration in the *Combined Flock Book* to all island breeders, a facility which no British breeder has ever enjoyed. Sadly, this offer was later turned down by the society, and there the matter rests.

Island Census

Although details of individual animals are not recorded, the society has organised a most useful breed census in the summer of 1987. The results, as set out in **Table 5**, show that there were 32 flocks in all, including the two museum flocks, with most having between five and 30 animals. A total of 349 ewes and 223 ewe lambs, makes a very healthy 572 females, a far cry from the figures of the 1950s. A ratio of 45 rams to 349 ewes, or one to eight, should ensure that a broad genetic base will avoid inbreeding. As only 20 of the 32 flocks have mature rams, the rest are presumably borrowing rams or cross breeding. Any further census could usefully clarify this point.

Table 5: Analysis of Flock Returns from the 1987 island census

Number of flocks relative to size

Flock size	1-5	6-10	11-20	21-50	51-75	76-100	101-200	201-300	**Total**
Number	7	10	7	5	0	2	0	1	**32**

Number of animals

Rams	Ram lambs	Ewes	Ewe lambs	Wethers	**Total**
45	18	349	223	99	**734**

Distribution of rams and ram lambs relative to flock size

Flock size	1-5	6-10	11-20	21-50	51-75	76-100	101-200	201-300
Rams	2	10	8	10	0	12	0	3
Ram lambs	1	1	7	6	0	3	0	0
Total	**3**	**11**	**15**	**16**	**0**	**15**	**0**	**3**

Flocks with rams (excluding ram lambs) — 20

Geographical distribution North-South division (Ramsey to Dalby)

	North	South	**Total**
Number of flocks	17	15	**32**
Number of sheep	249	485	**734**

The largest flock, in the 200-300 category, belongs of the Manx Museum.

The Loghtan as a symbol of 'Manxness'

The Loghtan ram has begun to replace the rather unimpressive Manx cat as a tourist symbol for the island. A ram figures prominently on the 1973 20p and current 5p Manx stamps (*Plates 79-80*), as it has done on their 1976 1p, 1980 5p and 1984 10p coins (*Plates 81-3*). Attractive printed designs on linen have been produced by Sheila Rowse for sale at a craft shop at Tynwald Mills (*Plate C20*). Postcards, coffee mugs and models featuring Loghtan rams are also available (*Plates 84-5*).

There is a small flock at Government House, the official residence of the island's Governor. This all helps to publicise the breed, both as a Manx national symbol and as a commercial asset. By organising good publicity, by staging a successful event each year and by involving highly placed members of the island's community in their events, the society has done much to promote the breed at home and abroad.

79. A ram on the Isle of Man 1973 20p stamp; twice actual size. (Photo by Dave Wicks; courtesy of Peter Wade-Martins)

80. A ram's head on the Isle of Man 5p stamp currently in circulation; twice actual size. (Photo by Dave Wicks; courtesy of Peter Wade-Martins)

81-3. Loghtan rams have been used three times in the Isle of Man coinage, although the design can be a little fanciful, with the ram on the 10p coin looking more like a unicorn; all twice actual size (Photos: 1p. by Dave Wicks, courtesy of Peter Wade-Martins; 5p. courtesy of the Manx Treasury; 10p. by Dave Wicks, courtesy of Peter Wade-Martins):

81. 1p (1976).

82. 5p (1980).

83. 10p (1984).

84. Porcelain model of a Loghtan produced by Shebeg Porcelain, Ballasalla, Isle of Man. (Photo by Dave Wicks, courtesy of Peter Wade-Martins)

Footnote

(1) THE MANX LOAGHTAN SHEEP BREED SOCIETY'S BREED CHARACTERISTICS

HEAD	Light boned, long and narrow from ears to muzzle, straight nose.
MUZZLE	Level jaws, neither protruding.
EYES	Bright and alert.
EARS	Small, short and strong, carried at 45'.
FACE	clean, with minimum of wool.
NECK	Medium length, head carried well above the top line.
SHOULDERS	Ram showing strength, Ewe light, in each case falling away slightly towards the ribs.
CHEST	Average to narrow, not outstanding or prominent.
BACK	Straight, level and of even width.
TAILHEAD	Continuation of top line.
TAIL	Well set in, not to reach the hocks nor to be below the bottom line, without wool for the greater part of its length.
HIND QUARTERS	Light and not too deeply fleshed.
LEGS	Long with light flat bone without wool from hocks to feet.

85. Coffee mug with Loghtan motif, made by Rushton Pottery, Tynwald Mills Craft Centre, Isle of Man. (Photo by Dave Wicks, courtesy of Peter Wade-Martins)

FEET	Very small and neat, pastern unobtrusive.
HORNS	Very dominant in rams. Proportionate to the size of the animal, two slightly curved primaries growing upwards and forward, two strong curved secondaries growing downward and forward, tertiaries are not unknown. Ewe has four finer curled horns, forward growing but not into the head.
FLEECE	About 3 lbs — 5 lbs in weight, staple 3"–5", very soft, close textured and lustrous, heavily oiled and excellent for hand spinning. Colour at birth, black or 'bitter chocolate' changing to lighter brown or coffee colour, bleaches in the sun. Loaghtan is Manx Gaelic for brown — from which the breed is named.

86. Air photograph of
Castlemilk Park in 1955, from
the south east. The 'golf
course', where the 'Shetlands'
usually grazed is the area of
parkland immediately beyond
the house. (Photo courtesy of the
Controller of HMSO: Crown
Copyright/RAF photograph)

C12. One of the author's rams, Longhouse Henry (L2596), which sired the 1989 RBST breed champion, Longhouse Ivor (L3320) (Plate 70). (Photo by Peter Wade-Martins)

C11. The Aldrich flock at Strathallan Castle in 1989. (Photo by Peter Wade-Martins)

C13. Left. 'Webbsgreen Cindy' (L2880), a ewe bred by John and Carole Keats at Soberton in Hampshire. It was the Primitive Breed Champion at the 1989 Singleton Rare Breeds Show. This ewe has a good brown face without the lighter areas around the eyes and under the chin, and it is of the type to be encouraged if the Castlemilk influence is to be reduced. (Photo courtesy of Carole Keats)

C14. A range of wool shades from Loghtan fleeces assembled by Carole Keats, who spins the wool and sells her woollen products under the name Webbs Green Farm Wool. (Photo by Edward Wade-Martins)

C15. Most Loghtan lambs are very dark, almost black, until their wool is bleached brown by the sun; occasionally, however, one appears with white patches on the face, on the legs and on the tip of the tail. This colour pattern can come from entirely brown parents, and does seem to be an ancient feature of the breed (see also Plate 56). (Photo by Peter Wade-Martins)

C16. There are increasingly classes for primitive breeds at agricultural shows. Here at the 1988 Singleton Rare Breeds Show five-year old Naomi Barcley is holding Bolney Melissa (L2946) which came first in her class of ewe lambs. (Photo courtesy of Jane Cooper)

C17. Two Island Heritage pullovers made of Loghtan wool. The darker one was made from wool put in a loft at Staward Farm in the Isle of Man in 1933 and recently discovered. It has a very dark gingery colour seldom seen in Loghtan fleeces today. The other is the colour of modern Loghtan wool. It may be that the old wool has darkened while in storage for 50 years. (Photo by Peter Wade-Martins)

C19. Above. A pullover knitted by Sue Leighton-White in Norfolk, a consultant in traditional hand knitting for the Wool Marketing Board. From the bottom of the pullover upwards, the following wools have been used: Merino cross, Loghtan carded with a little white Jacob, Loghtan carded with Hebridean, Merino cross and finally white Jacob. (Photo by Peter Wade-Martins)

C18. Left. Sheelagh Holmes wearing an Island Heritage jacket and skirt with her Loghtan flock. (Photo courtesy of Sheelagh Holmes)

C20. Left. A selection of items of printed linen designed by Sheila Rowse and sold at the Tynwald Mills craft centre, Isle of Man. (Photo by Peter Wade-Martins)

C21. Right. The flock of 'Shetlands' in Castlemilk Park in 1964. (Photo by Alastair Cameron, courtesy of Willie Morrison)

C22. A flock of Castlemilk Moorit sheep at Bagshot in Surrey owned by John Saunders, secretary of the Castlemilk Moorit Breeders Group.

The Origin of Castlemilk Moorits

The Castlemilk 'Shetland'

As this book has shown, the recent history of the Manx Loghtan and the origins of the Castlemilk Moorit are interlinked. To understand the Loghtan, one must try to establish the make-up of the Castlemilk.

The Castlemilk estate is set in the magnificent rolling scenery of Dumfriesshire, 4 km south of Lockerbie. Its unusual name comes from the river called the Water of Milk which flows past the Victorian castle.

This moorit-coloured sheep, which takes its name from the estate, is one of the rarest breeds in Britain. It was developed by Sir John Buchanan-Jardine who owned the estate for 42 years before he died in 1969. He ran the Home Farm more as a hobby than as a profit-making enterprise, and his two main interests were growing trees and livestock breeding. Under his stewardship thousands of trees were planted over the estate. Although self-taught, he became well known for his breeding of Galloway, Ayrshire and Guernsey cattle and the Dumfriesshire Foxhounds, which he originated.

There was a flock of 2-300 South Country Cheviots, and smaller flocks of Black Welsh Mountain sheep (which belonged to Lady Prudence, his second wife) and the 'Shetland' sheep. These 'Shetlands' were usually kept in a meadow in the park called the 'golf course' where they could be seen easily from the house (*Plate 86*). He had cloth made from their wool, and his son Sir Rupert still wears one of these jackets to this day. The estate cattle were well known at agricultural shows, and he was an acknowledged expert on foxhounds. By contrast, his breeding of the moorit-coloured 'Shetlands' was a rather personal and private affair, seen only by the few who ventured into the heavily wooded park. These sheep received very little publicity during his lifetime, gaining no more than passing comment in newspaper reports and magazine articles written about his farming activities.

Photographs of the flock are rare. Sir Rupert has a pair he took in the 1930s (*Plate 87*); a distant picture was published in an article on the Home Farm in *Farm and Country* in January 1960. There is also a pair of colour pictures taken in 1964 by the local doctor, Alastair Cameron, reproduced here (*Plates 88 and C21*). There is also a picture of two ewes taken soon after the residue of the flock reached the Cotswold Farm Park (*Plate 89*).

A cloud of uncertainty has surrounded the origins of the breed. Although Sir John always called them his 'Shetlands', it is certain that they were not just of Shetland stock. Their colour markings, their wool, their horn pattern and their size are significantly different from Shetlands; and they appear to have been derived from a variety of primitive short-tailed breeds. The Castlemilk Moorit, as it is called today, is now recognised as a breed by the Rare Breeds Survival Trust which has supported its revival. As it always breeds true, throwbacks which would help identify its predecessors do not occur. Speculation about the origins of the breed has been along the lines that it was created 'early this century' from a mixture of Shetland, Manx Loghtan and Soay, but until now there have been few hard facts to support these theories.

87. Two snapshots taken in the 1930's of the Castlemilk 'Shetlands' by Sir Rupert Buchanan-Jardine before his father had fixed the type of the breed. There are light and dark fleeces. Only some have 'Soay' markings and, most significant of all, one has white patches on the face as in some Manx Loghtans (Plate C15). These pictures provide further evidence of the close links between the Manx and Castlemilk breeds. (Photo by Sir Rupert Buchanan-Jardine)

Recent discoveries

Before Sir John inherited the estate from his father in 1927, he played little part in its management. He lived at Comlongen Castle overlooking the Solway Firth, 11 km to the south west, and leased the castle without land from Lord Mansfield. At that stage he had no opportunity to further his enthusiasm for livestock breeding, except for the foxhounds.

When Sir John did move to Castlemilk, it seems that he quickly became involved in its livestock management. He was a strongly independent man with his own views and his own ways. He enjoyed experimenting with livestock breeding and seldom left a breed as he found it. The herd of Galloway cattle he inherited was black, but after the war he decided to develop the rare dun-coloured strain, so that the whole herd of 230 cows became dun-coloured. The dairy herd of Ayrshires were dark brown, and the tan-coloured Dumfriesshire Foxhounds were bred to his own design. The breeding of all these are well recorded, but for his favourite sheep we have no such information, except for scraps of evidence recently gleaned from the estate records.

We are lucky that a very comprehensive series of letter books survives at the estate office from 1883 to modern times. These letters written by the factors over the period provide a glimpse of how a Victorian and Edwardian Scottish estate was managed. Their house in London, their racing stud at Newmarket, the management of the park and the Home Farm fill letter books with fascinating detail.

It may well be that it was his interest in brown-coloured livestock which attracted him to moorit-coloured Shetland sheep. In October 1928 he almost bought some Shetland ewe lambs being advertised by the Dupplin Castle estate near Perth. However, he preferred to buy mature stock, and the factor managed to obtain some for him in two consignments from a cattle dealer at Scalloway on Shetland. The first lot was paid for in November 1928 and the second in January 1930. The letters simply refer to moorit-coloured Shetlands, and the numbers involved are not mentioned. While it is clear that these two consignments provided the foundation stock for his breeding experiments, it is more difficult to identify the other breeds which were then used on them.

88. The flock of Castlemilk Moorits (or the 'Shetlands' as they were then called) in Castlemilk Park, 1964. (Photo by Dr. Alastair Cameron; courtesy of Willie Morrison)

On the Isle of Man we have two leads to help us. One is the memory that the father of the Kneale brothers at Ballacaley sent Loghtans to Castlemilk in the 1920s or 1930s (p.43). The other is the well documented fact that Edward Christian of Ballacallin said in October 1938 that he had imported two rams from Sir Buchanan-Jardine three years earlier (p.29). By searching the Castlemilk letter books of this period for copy letters indexed under 'Christian', it is possible to pick up the Castlemilk side of the story.

Edward Christian first contacted the estate through his sister in Carlisle in November 1933. Then, there is a gap in the record while Sir John and Edward Christian were corresponding direct. However, in October 1936 there is a letter from the factor to Edward Christian confirming arrangements for the delivery of a ram *to* Lockerbie station. It is obvious that the two men actually swapped rams. Perhaps the ram Edward Christian sent to Lockerbie was from Ballacaley[1].

In August 1934 the factor wrote to the Secretary of the Wiltshire Horn Sheep Society saying that Sir John had been crossing their breed with the Shetlands, and 'the result was that we got a very good fleece which is what Sir John wishes'. What we can make of that is another matter, since the Wiltshire Horn is the one British sheep breed without a woollen fleece.

There is then a gap in our knowledge of his breeding programme. The fact that the sheep were already grazing on the 'golf course' by 1930 is, however, confirmed by a living eye witness, Hugh Spence, now retired and living in Lockerbie. He grew up at Cowdens, one of the tenant farms, and as a boy walked regularly through the park to school. The shepherd at the time was called John Beattie. The next shepherd was Tom Swan, and then came Willie Morrison, who was estate shepherd from 1949 until he retired in 1971. Willie Morrison still lives in the estate village of Kettleholm, and has clear memories of Sir John's 'Shetlands'. He recalls how Sir John always personally selected the ewe lambs and tups for breeding, and that the rejects were then dispatched to the local butcher. He is quite certain that during the time he was shepherd no outside stock was ever introduced into the flock. It remained a closed flock from at least 1949 until it was partly dispersed but mainly slaughtered in 1970, when Sir Rupert was putting the management of the estate on a more economic footing.

89. The first published picture of Castlemilk Moorit ewes at the Cotswold Farm Park about 1973, as printed in the 1975 Combined Flock Book. *(Photo courtesy of Countrywide Livestock Ltd.)*

The flock usually consisted of about 60 ewes and two to three rams, and they lambed at about 140%. Neither Willie Morrison nor Sir John kept records, so it would not have been possible to devise a carefully structured mating programme to minimise the effects of inbreeding. The flock was therefore clearly very inbred, but nevertheless remained strong and vigorous right up to the end. This must be why Joe Henson and the Rare Breeds Survival Trust were able to revive the breed from the one ram and nine ewes without having to depend on the outcrosses which were created as a safely measure.

Although outside blood was not introduced in the 1950s, we know that Sir John did consider doing so. On the Isle of Man, Jack Quine's old calendars record that in November 1955 one or more sheep were dispatched by the Manx Museum to Castlemilk (p.47). At the Castlemilk end, five copy letters to Major Brownsdon sent in the period of October and November that year set out the arrangements for the transfer. Sir John had asked for a swap as before, but that proved impossible because Major Brownsdon had decided to fix the Manx Museum sheep as a four-horned flock. A crate for the ram was dispatched to the Isle of Man, and on 21st November the factor was able to write confirming that the animal had arrived safely.

Willie Morrison remembers the ram well; it was four-horned, and after a while the top horns had to be cut back so that it could graze. He is absolutely sure, however, that the ram was never used. Why it wasn't he doesn't remember, although it may be that as Sir John had asked for a two-horned animal he didn't want to see the Castlemilk sheep become a four-horned breed.

Willie Morrison also remembers that a pair of dark Soay tup lambs arrived at some stage; they were put to three or four ewes, but they and their offspring were also discarded without contributing to the flock. Joe Henson, in his article on the breed published in *The Ark* in May 1985, says that he had understood a Soay ram was used but rejected because the progeny were too small. These two stories sound as though they are describing the same event. Current theories about the origins of the breed are surely derived from these episodes in the 1950s, but we now know that the breed had been fixed well before then, probably in the 1930s.

It is encouraging to see that the breed has been revived, when it came closer to extinction even than the Loghtans. In his 1985 article, Joe Henson finishes with these words:

90. A Castlemilk Moorit ram at the 1988 R.B.S.T. Show and Sale, again exhibiting the distinctive light Castlemilk markings under the chin, around the eyes on the belly and down the inside of the legs. The breed also has a light area around the tail, as in Plate C22. (Photo by Peter Wade-Martins)

When you consider the breed's present secure position in the light of its near extinction at the time of the dispersal at Castlemilk it gives you cause to wonder. It also gives encouragement to those breeds which might find themselves in similar circumstances in the future anywhere in the world.

A breed developed to beautify the park at Castlemilk and provide wool for the Buchanan-Jardine family is now spread throughout the land from the Isle of Coll to Devon and Kent. Its fine, kemp-free moorit wool, chocolate brown underneath and bleached a pale fawn on top is much sought after by spinners, and has recently attracted the attention of a professional weaving mill, producing quality cloth. The sheep are hardy and self reliant and rarely suffer from foot rot. The ewes milk well and are exceptionally protective mothers. Woe betide any un-suspecting dog or fox which goes near a Moorit with young lambs. The wethers provide a fat-free carcass whose tender flesh is more akin to venison than mutton.

But for all its commercial attributes, to me, as I stand in the failing evening light after the Farm Park has closed admiring my Moorit flock, its beauty is always paramount.

The successful restoration of the Castlemilk against all the odds has indeed been an inspiration to us all.

Conclusions

In summary, we now know the Castlemilk Moorit breed was based on two consignments of Shetlands which had arrived on the estate by 1930 and that a Manx Loghtan ram was introduced in 1936. What other breeds contributed to the flock has not yet been established, although the use of a Soay remains a strong possibility. Its arrival may be recorded somewhere in the estate office letter books. The problem is that for the period in question (1927-1949) these books contain more than 60,000 letters. Without a lead, such as a date or the name of the supplier, the right letter would be a veritable needle in a haystack. Perseverance, however, may reap its reward one day.

91. Castlemilk Moorit ram M0145. Notice how similar the face and horns are to the rams in Plates 24 & 94. (Photo by Howard Payton; courtesy of Bridget Parke)

Footnote

(1) There seems to be no correspondence with Sir Mark Collet who also said he had imported a Castlemilk ram to the Isle of Man. However, this is not necessarily significant since he would probably have used an agent to organise any purchase of livestock.

A Time to Reflect

The past

The publication of this history of the Manx Loghtan breed coincides with the formation of the Manx Loghtan Sheep Breeders Group of the Rare Breeds Survival Trust (*Plate 93*). This final chapter allows us to reflect on how it is the breed has ever survived and on the characters of the people to whom we are indebted for its survival. It is a fascinating story of sheep and shepherds. Some parts are well recorded; others are surrounded with uncertainty even for quite recent periods. Memories fade fast when one has to delve back more than 30 years, and it is important that the threads are pulled together while people who were crucial to the breed's survival are still with us. This book is dedicated to all who figure in this story. Without their endeavours we would not today have a breed of sheep which has created so much interest amongst rare breed enthusiasts.

The Manx Loghtan is all we have left of a small primitive breed of mountain sheep which probably covered the hills of Man in their thousands until the eighteenth century. They were generally white, but many were grey, some were black and only just a few were Loghtan-coloured. Knitted socks and cloth garments made of Loghtan wool were highly prized. As the numbers of mountain sheep dwindled, there was some attempt to select for the Loghtan-coloured fleece, and when there were only a few animals left the Loghtan colour predominated.

They were both two- and four-horned. It is sometimes claimed today that Manx Loghtans have to be four-horned, but all the existing and extinct polycerate (multi-horned) breeds in north-west Europe have been mixed two- and four-horned stock. Records from the last 100 years demonstrate beyond doubt that both types of horn pattern should be accepted for this breed.

In these pages we have covered the history of the breed from as far back as we can trace it through to the present day. That we have a Manx Loghtan at all is a miracle. From the middle of the eighteenth century the breed had become largely irrelevant to the farming needs of the island. By the late nineteenth century its survival was dependent upon a succession of enthusiasts who at various stages took over the depleted stock and nurtured it while those around them saw little sense in perpetuating a breed which did not suit current farming practices.

The breed was renowned for its ability to survive on poor upland grazing. When it was brought down to lower ground in winter, it was expected to survive without much access to hay and had to scavenge for weeds and edible roots where it could. The mothering instinct of the ewes was well known, and the mutton was an epicure's delight.

Despite these advantages, the need for a longer-stapled white fleece and for breeds which produced faster-maturing lambs counted for more in the eighteenth and nineteenth centuries. The woollen industry was becoming mechanised, and the drive for farm improvement was everywhere to be seen.

In the midst of all this, we have Robert Quirk, a very traditional farmer who was convinced that old breeds of livestock and long-cherished farming methods were the best. He was not going to modernise just because everyone

92. The first step in the formation of a Loghtan breeder's group was a Breeder's Workshop held at the National Agricultural Centre at Stoneleigh in May 1987. Part of the day's programme was devoted to a discussion of breed characteristics when Barbara Platt, one of the first people to have Loghtans in Britain, explained the finer points of the breed using sheep from the NAC Loghtan flock. (Photo by Mike Naughton; courtesy of the Rare Breeds Survival Trust)

else was, and he held on to his mountain breed. Then came Captain Windus and Colonel Anderson who spotted Quirk's sheep and bought some, perhaps as a novelty.

Caesar Bacon was next, and he towers above most other people associated with the preservation of the breed. He was clearly a modern-day farmer and was from a long line of Bacons interested in model farming. He had a fine flock of Shropshires, much in demand amongst commercial farmers of his day. His herd of Longhorn cattle were some of the best on the island. But, despite all this, he took a passionate interest in the survival of these little primitive sheep which came from an earlier age.

Bacon, as far as we can tell, bought up what was left of Robert Quirk's flock to start a breeding programme. The stock was no doubt inbred, and the numbers were too low to maintain the breed without introducing some outside blood. He then travelled the Hebrides, the Shetlands, the Faroes and Iceland studying the short-tailed sheep of the North West, and chose the Shetland with its excellent wool and moorit colour to cross with his Manx mountain sheep.

Bacon's flock book is a most careful record of his breeding programme, and when he sold stock he wrote out a pedigree for each animal. The quality of his recording was not equalled until 1974 when Countrywide Livestock Ltd. set up the *Combined Flock Book* for rare breeds of sheep. Indeed, until then none of Bacon's successors ever kept detailed records as far as we know, and certainly not the Manx Museum.

The animal Bacon produced, as depicted in the painting he presumably commissioned, was partly his creation: a Manx-Shetland cross of pure, or almost pure, Loghtan colouring. The horn pattern and the short tight fleece are undoubtedly more Manx than Shetland, and it seems that he was able to devise a breeding programme to minimise the long-term effect of the Shet-

93. The breed promotion stand
organised by the newly-
formed Group won first prize
for the best stand at the 1988
Show and Sale. The stand had
been sponsored by Costains,
the building contractors.
(Photo by Peter Wade-Martins)

land blood in the stock he produced. Calculations based on his flock book show that the lambs born in the period 1901-7 were 94% Manx. Indeed, one would not know today, but for his records and the accounts of his contemporaries, that the breed has Shetland blood in its ancestry.

Bacon's death at the age of only 46 in 1916 could have been the end of the breed. Fortunately, the distribution of breeding stock through his annual sales to several breeders in different parts of the island ensured its survival during the difficult years ahead. He had built up a small group of enthusiasts amongst the farming community — in particular, Thomas Quirk, J. Q. Cannell and Edward Christian — who regarded themselves after his death as his successors. They kept the breed going during the 1920s and 1930s, assisted by Mrs Moore and latterly by Mrs Lascelles. Once again, there was an injection of outside blood, this time from the Castlemilk flock in Dumfriesshire, although why that was necessary then is not clear. The overall flock size should have been sufficient for them to maintain the breed without this if they had been better organised. Two or three Castlemilk rams were used by at least two of the breeders in the 1930s and 1940s. This rather crude use of imported rams year after year must have introduced much more Shetland blood into the genetic make-up of the breed than did Bacon's careful breeding programme 40 years earlier.

When these breeders died or gave up farming as war approached there was no-one ready to step into their shoes. Once again, the breed was in real danger. Then somehow, and *how* is not recorded, a retired farmer in his 70s from Kent named Sir Mark Collet, who was building a mansion for himself on the island, saw there was a need for the breed to be protected. He arranged for a Ramsey auctioneer to collect together surviving animals off the farms. The flock he assembled then grazed in the fields around his new house at Ballamanaugh in Sulby and on the hills nearby. The Sulby area, just below the Manx mountains, was, it seems, the traditional home of this mountain breed: it was where this century farmers have seemed least willing to give them up altogether. Two other small and less publicised flocks were also maintained nearby, at Staward and Ballacaley, and there was a fourth at Strathallan Castle in Port St. Mary.

We know nothing of Collet's management of the flock, except that he also imported a Castlemilk ram. This time we have pictures of the ram and its progeny, and we can see from the strong 'Soay' markings on his offspring that the ram did have a very significant impact on the appearance of the flock at the time. By 1953 his second- or third- generation offspring actually looked more like Castlemilk Moorit than Manx.

However, the flocks at Ballacaley and Strathallan were not, as far as we know, dependent on the museum flock for a ram until Nellie Keig had one from the museum sometime after 1955. So, the impact of the Castlemilk Moorits may well in the long term not be as great as seemed likely in 1953: it is probable (but not proven) that a Ballacaley ram was used on the museum flock from 1953. Since 1972 a ram lamb from the Strathallan flock has gone back into the museum flock's gene pool each year, thus significantly diluting the Castlemilk influence still further.

Between the 1930s and the 1950s, the genetic make-up of the island's flocks had been more influenced by outside stock than Bacon ever allowed it to be. The 'Soay' markings especially apparent on the Calf flock today are more likely to be derived from the Castlemilk influence than the effects of the later limited use of the one short-lived Soay ram.

When the Manx Museum took over Sir Mark's flock in 1953 there were no more than perhaps 75 Loghtan ewes in total on the island. The museum then cut its own numbers from 35 down to 12 when the flock moved to Druidale. With hindsight, this rather ruthless culling and the museum's decision not to expect Major Brownsdon to keep more than 12 ewes could easily have led to the extinction of the breed, especially with their flock being so heavily inbred. The ram died and ewe numbers dwindled lower during the 1950s, when the breed total for the island may have been as low as 20 or 30. But for the determination of Jack Quine, the breed would have gone under, because Nellie Keig could not have sustained the breed unaided and there was too much cross-breeding going on at Ballacaley. Few other breeds have come so close to extinction and survived.

The museum's decision to import a Soay ram in 1966 was also most unwise, and we must be thankful it died. It would have been more sensible to establish a well-organised breeding programme for the remaining animals on the island. The Whipsnade animals were available; failing all that, the moorit Shetland would have been far more appropriate if outside blood had to be used.

The fact that neither the museum nor the Strathallan flocks have ever been recorded means that historians of the breed are working at a great disadvantage. But in practice, recording by itself would not have improved the breed's chances of survival unless expertise in the field of genetics had been used to oversee a breeding programme when numbers were so critically low.

Thanks to the endeavours of first Colby Cubbin and then Nellie Keig there was a small flock running parallel to, but separate from, the museum flock up to the 1960s. But for them, the breed as we know it today would be more Castlemilk than Manx.

By the late 1960s all was well again, and from then on numbers rose; the creation from some of the best museum animals available of a reserve flock at

94. The author with his ram Alfred (L430) in 1987. (Photo by Edward Wade-Martins)

the Sheep Unit of the National Agricultural Centre at Stoneleigh in War-wickshire was a wise move. Alastair Dymond, then in charge of the Unit, must be given full credit for this initiative. Not only did it ensure against further disasters, it also helped to encourage outside interest in the breed with the consequent proliferation of further breeding units all over the British Isles.

The present

If Caesar Bacon could look down upon us now he should feel well pleased. The breed, much as he fashioned it, is alive and well and in numbers he could never have dreamed of. There are flocks in most corners of Britain, thanks to the Manx Museum and the Rare Breeds Survival Trust. The British flocks are now well recorded, although breeders on the Isle of Man are still reluctant to join the Trust's recording scheme. There is an enthusiastic Manx Loghtan Sheep Breeders Group formed under the wing of the R.B.S.T., and there are now much happier relations between Manx and British breeders. On the island the two museum flocks are strong and healthy. The island's Manx Loghtan Sheep Breed Society has members sufficient to support an annual Loghtan Sheep Fair, and the Manx awareness of its native breed has been much heightened by the Society's well placed publicity.

Both the island society and the British group have the same message to convey to the sheep world, that is: here we have a small hardy attractive breed, which has amazingly good mothering instincts, which very seldom suffers from footrot, fly-strike or mastitis, which has few lambing problems and which has a proven ability to produce quality cross-bred lambs effi-ciently. Because the ewe is small it is possible to have a high stocking rate. The system also benefits from the hardiness of the mother, the amazing (some would say explosive) hybrid vigour of the cross-bred lamb and the meat qualities of the ram. Such a statement may seem too good to be true; nevertheless, it is a fact that, due to the prepotency of the male, the lambs inherit the appearance of their sires much more than their dams. When the system is measured in terms of kg. of meat per hectare of grass, the results

101

95. Some of the ewes in the author's flock at North Elmham, Norfolk, 1987 (Photo by Peter Wade-Martins)

show that there are few systems to rival it. The R.B.S.T. is funding trials on a number of different farms where Loghtans are being directly compared with half-breed ewes using the same terminal sire. Early indications are that on a gross margin per hectare the Loghtans will outstrip the half-breds.

In 1987 it was a Loghtan fleece which won the overall championship in the Rare Breeds fleece competition at Stoneleigh. The wool, although it does have a shorter staple than the Shetland, is attractive and can be spun by itself or with longer-stapled wools to make various shades of brown. For those breeders who produce pure-bred stock, there is the added pleasure of having lean meat full of flavour for the freezer which few other breeds can rival. No other joint of meat can possibly taste as good as a leg from an over-yeared Loghtan wether. The claim David Robertson made in 1794 that the Manx sheep were 'perhaps the most delicious in the world' rings as true today as it did then.

The future

It is difficult to foretell the future of the breed, especially in a book where research has been aimed at looking backwards rather than forwards. Nevertheless, at a time when more and more people not experienced in livestock farming would like to have a few acres of land on which to graze some sheep, using an easy-to-manage system, the Loghtan is an obvious choice. For the quality lamb producer it has great potential; an advantage of 13-14% more carcass weight per acre over Mules is a remarkable asset.

At the last count, there were over 600 females on the island and about 700 in Britain. **Table 1** shows how the quantities of stock and the numbers of breeders have increased over the last 15 years. Growth has slowed down while breeders have experimented with cross breeding, but the trend is still upward. Whether the breed will ever have any large-scale commercial application will depend on a scientific demonstration of its potential as a commercial meat producer from more extensive trials. These are now surely required so that its cross-breeding performance can be accurately measured against that of more fashionable varieties.

The Knockaloe Experimental Farm near Peel on the Isle of Man, with its flock of Scottish Half-bred ewes and pedigree Suffolks could be the ideal body to experiment on the island; the R.A.S.E.'s Sheep Unit at Stoneleigh could be a suitable location in Britain. Certainly, the R.B.S.T.'s current small-scale experiments need to be repeated using much larger numbers.

If a breakthrough can also be made into the field of commercial fat lamb production, then, who knows, perhaps one day some of the fields of familiar white sheep may change to a gentler shade of brown.

Sources

Bibliography

Alderson, G.L.H., 1977. 'Comparative performance standards for some minority breeds of sheep', *The Ark* IV (7), 227-232.

Alderson, G.L.H., 1978. 'Rare breeds in the British sheep industry', *The Ark* V (6), 195-198.

Alderson,G.L.H.,1980. 'Inheritance of the polycerate characteristic: an interim report', *The Ark* VII (10), 332.

Alderson, G.L.H., 1985. 'Selection methods and breeding programmes used in the conservation of rare breeds of coloured sheep', *The Ark* XII (12), 424-426.

Alderson, G.L.H., 1986. 'Coloured sheep and their potential value', *The Ark* XIII (3), 87-91.

Alderson, G.L.H., 1986. 'Combined Flock Book', *The Ark* XIII (10), 336-339.

Alderson, G.L.H., 1987. 'Manx Loghtan breeder's workshop', *The Ark* XIV (6), 192-193.

Aldington, A., 1989. *A History of the Jacob Sheep*

Allen, D., 1989. 'Its the return of the super sheep!', *Cumberland News Autumn Agricultural Review.*

Anon, 1862. Note under the heading of 'Extra-ordinary Fecundity', *Mona's Herald*, 5th February 1862, referring to a short note headed 'Prolific Manx Sheep' in the previous week's edition.

Anon, 1867. 'On the Breeding and Management of Sheep in the Isle of Man'. (B225 Manx Museum)

Anon, 1912. *A Guide to Domesticated Animals*, British Museum (Natural History), 13 & fig.7.

Anon, 1932. 'Kent education remodelled', *Kent Messenger*

Anon, 1952. 'The Manx Loghtan sheep an interesting old breed', *Ramsey Courier* 18 January 1952.

Anon, 1960. 'Castlemilk farms: the breeding projects of Sir John Buchanan-Jardine', *Farm and Country* 6 January.

Anon, 1975. 'Farm of the month: The National Agricultural Centre', *The Ark* II (1), 6-8.

Anon, 1975. 'Registration programme No.4: Manx Loghtan sheep', *The Ark* II (5), 107.

Anon, 1975. 'Farm of the month: Chapel Cottage', *The Ark* II (9), 216-217.

Anon, 1977. 'Breed of the month', *The Ark*, IV (1), 6-7.

Anon, 1979. 'Manx Loghtan exports', *The Ark* VI (12), 306.

Anon, 1983. 'Breed accepted', *The Ark* X (12), 422-3.

Anon, 1985. 'Combined Flock Book', *The Ark* XII (1), 8-10.

Anon, 1989. 'Manx Loghtan registrations', *The Ark* XVI (2), 40.

Bazin, F. (ed.), 1984. *The Manx Loaghtan Sheep, the breed that refused to die* (Manx Loaghtan Sheep Breed Society).

Bazin, M.J.C., 1988. 'Manx Loaghtan Sheep Breed Society 1987 Census of island flock', *The Ark* XV (4), 115.

Blundell, W.,1876. 'A history of the Isle of Man', written 1648-1656, Harrison, W. (ed.), *Manx Society* XXV and XXVI,43.

Bowie, S.H.V., 1987. 'Shetland's native farm animals: Shetland sheep', *The Ark* XIV (6), 194-199.

Briggs, H., 1988. 'The sheep that refused to die', *Isle of Man Examiner* 25 October.

Briggs, H., 1989a. 'Old painting may provide clues', *Isle of Man Examiner*, 16 May.

Briggs, H., 1989b. 'Mystery remains over painting', *Isle of Man Examiner*, 20 June.

Briggs, J.K., 1976. 'More about Manx', *The Ark* III (2), 56-7.

Brownsdon, T.E., 1956. 'The Loghtan', *Spillers Livestock Magazine* No 62, 21.

Brownsdon, T.E., 1964. 'An Historical Note on Manx Agriculture,' *Isle of Man Natural History and Antiquarian Society Proceedings* VII, No.1, 5-12.

Buchanan-Jardine, J., 1937 *Hounds of the World*

Caine, P.W., 1931. (presumed to be by Caine) 'The Manx native sheep, its cross with the by Faroe Breed', *Isle of Man Weekly Times*,10th January 1931.

Caine, P.W., 1938. 'The Loaghtan sheep. old Manx breed, rare but surviving', *Isle of Man Weekly Times* 15th October 1938.

Camden, W., 1772. Gibson, Bp. (ed.), *Britannia*, 392.

Collet, M.,1945. 'Manx', *The Countryman* Autumn 1945, 38.

Collet, M.,1946. 'Interesting article by the late Sir Mark Collet', *Isle of Man Courier* January 1946.

Crowe, W.I.C., 1975. 'Manx Loaghtyn sheep'', *The Ark* II (11), 302-303.

Danjalsson A Ryggi, M., 1935. *Dyralaera* I, Sugdyr, 75-76 (Foraya Laerarafelag, Torshavn).

Dymond, A., 1979. 'Minority Breeds at the NAC', *The Ark* VI (9), 277-278.

Dymond, A., 1988. 'Manx matters', *The Ark* XV (10), 367-8.

Elwes, H.J., 1912. 'Notes on the primitive breeds of sheep in Scotland', *The Scottish Naturalist* No 3, 49-51.

Elwes, H.J.,1913. *Guide to the Primitive Breeds of Sheep and their Crosses, with Notes on the Management of*

Park Sheep in England (republished by the Rare Breeds Survival Trust, 1983), 22-23 and Figs. 12-15 and 17.

Ewart, J.C., 1913-14. 'Domestic sheep and their wild ancestors', *Transactions of the Highland Agricultural Society of Scotland* 25, 160-190; 26, 74-101.

Garrad, L., 1986. 'The Manx Loghtan' in Harrison, S. (ed.) *100 Years of Heritage, the work of the Manx Museum and National Trust* (Manx Museum and National Trust), 130-133.

Gosset, A.L.J., 1911. *Shepherds of Britain, scenes from shepherd life past and present*, 62-69.

Hall, S., 1987. 'Breed structures and conservation of Portland, Manx Loghtan and Hebridean sheep', *The Ark* XIV (5), 154-157.

Henson, E., 1981. 'A study of the congenital defect 'split eyelid' in the multi-horned breeds of British sheep', *The Ark* VIII (3), 84-90.

Henson, E.L., 1981. 'Manx Loghtans on the Isle of Man', *The Ark* VIII (4), 125-128.

Henson, J., 1985. 'Castlemilk Moorit sheep', *The Ark* XII (5), 169-171.

Holmes, S., 1985. 'Wool gathering', *The Ark* XII (6), 204-205.

Hunt, J., 1989. 'Prices soar for rare breeds', *Farmers Weekly* 111 (11), 93.

Jeffcot, J.M., 1890. 'Address of the retiring president, High-Bailiff of Castletown', *Yn Lioar Manninagh* I (5), 153-158.

Jewell, P., 1980. 'The Soay sheep', *The Ark* VII (2), 51-57; VII (3), 87-93.

Lascelles, F.M., 1955. Typed manuscript entitled 'Loaghtyn Veg' by Mrs Lascelles, undated but catalogued as 1955 (MS 5575B, Manx Museum).

Kinvig, R.H., 1975. *The Isle of Man: a social, cultural and political history*.

Lydekker, R., 1912. *The Sheep and its Cousins*, 61-62.

Moorhouse, S., 1953. 'Reclamation work in the Isle of Man', *Sport and Country* 195, No. 3837, 21 January, 54-5.

Noddle, B., 1974. 'The early history of sheep', *The Ark* I (2), 14-15.

Noddle, B. 1977. 'The early history of the sheep', *The Sheep Farmer* (Summer), 16-22.

Noddle, B., 1978. 'Some minor skeletal differences in sheep', *Research Problems in Zooarchaeology* 133-141.

Noddle, B.A., 1980. 'Polycerate sheep', *The Ark* VII (5), 156-164.

Olner, J., 1954. *An Account of Sheep Farming Practise in the Isle of Man*. Unpublished thesis submitted towards a B.Sc. Degree (Hons.) in the Faculty of Agriculture, King's College, University of Durham (recently mislaid: no longer available).

Parkinson, R., 1810. *Treatise on the Breeding and Management of Livestock, in which the principles and proceedings of the new school of breeders are fully and experimentally discussed* I, 252: II, 5 (Cambridge University Library rare books room).

Platt, B., 1976. 'Opinions on ram numbers and Manx Loghtans', *The Ark* III (1), 24-5.

Porter, V., 1987. *Practical Rare Breeds*, 179-181.

Quayle, T., 1812. *General View of Agriculture of the Isle of Man*, 111-116.

Roberts, J.A.F. and White, R. G., 1930. 'Colour inheritance in Sheep IV', *Journal of Genetics* 22 (2), 165-180.

Roberts, J.A.F. and White, R.G., 1930. 'Colour inheritance in Sheep IV', *Journal of Genetics* 22 (2), 165-180.

Robertson, D., 1794. *A Tour through the Isle of Man*, reprinted 1970.

Rogers, A., 1987. 'Dressed to kilt', *Farmers Weekly* 107, 4 Dec, inside back cover.

Ryder, M.L., 1964. 'The History of Sheep Breeds in Britain', *Agricultural History Review* 12 (1), 1-12; (2), 65-82.

Ryder, M.L., 1968. 'The evolution of Scottish breeds of sheep', *Scottish Studies* 12, 127-167.

Ryder, M.L., 1983. *Sheep and Man*

Sacheverell, W., 1702. *A Short Survey of the Isle of Man*, 4.

Stenning, E.H., 1958. *Portrait of the Isle of Man*, 131.

Trow-Smith, R., 1957. *A History of British Livestock Husbandry to 1700*.

Wade-Martins, P., 1986. 'Breeding Manx Loghtans: is it worth it?', *The Ark* XIII (5), 168-171.

Wade-Martins, P., 1988. 'Loghtans of the Isle of Man', *The Ark* XV (3), 88-93.

Wallace, R., 1907. *Farm Livestock of Great Britain*, 519-526.

Watson, J.M., 1978. 'Split eyelids', *The Ark* V (12), 428-429.

Werner, A.R., 1977. 'Hebridean (St. Kilda) sheep', *The Ark* IV (7), 224-225.

White, R.G., 1950. 'Manx Loghtan sheep', *Manx Journal of Agriculture* July, 25-6.

Whitehead, G.K., 1954. 'The Manx Loghtan sheep', *Country Life* 4th March 1954, 594-595 (reproduced in *Manx Journal of Agriculture* VIII (1954), 19-27; republished without reference to its original date with new photographs in *The Ark* V (1978), 371-374).

Williamson, K., 1945. Article in *The Peregrine* I, No. 3 (September 1945) makes reference to Caesar Bacon crossing sheep from Faroes.

Woods, G.,1811. *An Account of the Past and Present State of the Isle of Man; including a Topographical Description; a Sketch of its Mineralogy; An Outline of its Laws, with the Privilege enjoyed by Strangers; and a History of the Island*, 41-2.

Youatt, W., 1837. *Sheep, their Breeds, Management and Diseases*, 301.

Other references etc.

Advertisements, notices and reports relating to Caesar Bacon's annual sales in the Isle of Man Weekly Times 26 Sept. 1896, p.8, col.2; 3 Oct. 1896, p.8, col.3; 24 Sept. 1896, p.8, col.3; 16 Sept. 1899, p.8, col.4; 30 Sept. 1899. p.5, col.6; 29 Sept. 1900, p.12, col.2; 13 Oct. 1900, p.12, col.1; 20 Oct. 1900, p.9, col.4; 28 Sept. 1901, p.8, col.1; 5 Oct. 1901, p.7, col.7; 27 Sept. 1902, p.8, col.1; 4 Oct. 1902, p.9, col.4; 3 Oct. 1903, p.8, col.1; 10 Oct. 1903, p.5, col.1; 1 Oct. 1904, p.3, col.4; 8 Oct. 1904, p.7, col.5; 15 Oct. 1904, p.7, col.5; 21 Oct. 1905, p.8, col.1; 6 Oct. 1906, p.8, col.2; 13 Oct. 1906, p.7, col.6; 5 Oct. 1907, p.8, col.1; 5 Oct. 1907, p.7, col.2; 12 Oct. 1907, p.5, col.7; 10 Oct. 1908, p. 8, col.1; 17 Oct. 1908, p.6, col.8; 2 Oct. 1909, p.8, col.2; 16 Oct. 1909, p.9, col.7; 15 Oct. 1910, p.9, col.4; 8 Oct. 1911, p.8, col.1; 14 Oct. 1911, p.7, col.4; 9 Nov. 1912, p.8, col.1; 16 Nov. 1912, p.7, col.4; 22 Nov. 1913, p.8, col. 1; 29 Nov. 1913, p.7, col.5; 5 Dec. 1914, p.8, col.1; 12 Dec. 1914, p.8, col.7; 4 Dec. 1915, p.8, col.1; 11 Dec. 1915, p.5, col.6.

Death of John Joseph Bacon
Memorial notice of John Joseph Bacon, died 9th March 1909, *Manx Quarterly* No.6 (May 1909), 589.

Reports of the Isle of Man Agricultural Show in the Isle of Man Weekly Times 3 Aug. 1895, p.5; 8 Aug. 1896, p.5; 7 Aug. 1897, p.4; 6 Aug. 1898, p.3; 12 Aug. 1899, p.8; 11 Aug. 1900, p.7; 10 Aug. 1901, p.4; 9 Aug. 1902, p.2; 8 Aug. 1903, p.3; 6 Aug. 1904, p.4; 22 Jul. 1905, p.5; 11 Aug. 1906. p.8; 10 Aug 1907, p.8; 9 Aug. 1908, p.7; 7 Aug. 1909, p.4; 6 Aug. 1910, p.3; 12 Aug. 1911, p. 3; 10 Aug. 1912, p.2; 9 Aug. 1913, p.9; 8 Aug. 1914, p.2; 7 Aug. 1915, p.2; 5 Aug. 1916, p. 5; 9 Aug. 1919, p.2.

Death of J. Caesar Bacon
Memorial notice of J. Caesar Bacon, died 11th May 1916, *Manx Quarterly* No.17 October 1916, 56.

Report of funeral the previous Monday at Onchan church: *Isle of Man Weekly Times* 20 May 1916, p.9, col.2: and notice of death p.5, col.6.

Obituaries in *Isle of Man Examiner* 13 May 1916, p.4, col.4 and *Mona's Herald* 17 May 1916, p.6, col.6.

Advertisements and reports relating to Caesar Bacon's dispersal sales examined in the Isle of Man Weekly Times 20 May 1916, p.8, col.4; 27 May 1916, p.8, cols.4&5; 10 June 1916, p.11, col.3; 17 June 1916, p.11, col.4; 29 July, 1916, p.8, col.3.

Reports of the Southern Agricultural Show in the Isle of Man Weekly Times 14 Aug. 1920, p.7; 13 Aug. 1921, p.7; 12 Aug. 1922, p.7; 11 Aug. 1923, p.9; 16 Aug. 1924, p.7; 15 Aug. 1925, p.4; 14 Aug. 1926, p.6; 13 Aug. 1927, p.4; 18 Aug. 1928, p.9; 17 Aug. 1929, p.9; 9 Aug. 1930, p.8; 15 Aug. 1931, p.8; 13 Aug. 1932, p.10; 19 Aug. 1933, p.8; 18 Aug. 1934, p. 7; 17 Aug. 1935, p.7.

Mounted specimens in the Manx Museum
Complete adult sheep (IOMMM 3822) donated in 1937 by James Brew, a Ramsey Butcher.

Lamb (IOMMM 3618) bred 1935/6 by Mrs Lascelles at Baldroma, Maughold.

Ram head (IOMMM 6250) from Major Bacon's Seafield flock, donated 1950 by Mr. Kinvig.

Ram skull (IOMMM 3726), donated 1936/7, from Mrs Riggall's flock at Great Meadow.

Ewe's head (IOMMM 3363), donated 1934/5, from a 7-year old ewe bred by F.W. Quirk at Ballawattleworth.

Other items in the Manx Museum
Carriage rug (IOMMM 5018) from Mrs E.M. Gawne of Kentraugh; a wedding present to the donor's mother, Sophia Powys, in 1878. Donor: Mrs W.H.B. Somerset 21.4.39.

Carriage rug (IOMMM 55-162) from the Gawnes of Kentraugh *c.* 1870. Donor: Mr. E.C. Ruscoe 4.5.55.

Quilt (IOMMM 72-210A) from the Harrison family of Ballakindry, Arbory, probably *c.* 1880-1890.

Mounted specimens in British Museum (Natural History)
Complete Loghtan 4-horned adult ram (1980.2592,S14) presented by Bacon in 1901 (right ear punched as for ear tag and torn).

Complete Loghtan 2-horned adult ewe (1980.2593,S75) presented by Elwes in 1914 (right ear has a semicircular notch on lower side). The horn shape is not quite right for this to be the ewe shown in Elwes (1913), fig. 15.

Mounted piebald 4-horned ram's head (1980.2591,S54) from Rowland Ward, taxidermist, in 1926. Breed unknown; possibly Jacob or less likely a Loghtan: there is some brown around the eyes.

Other Papers
Caesar Bacon's flock book covering the period 1895-1907, MS 5188 in the Manx Museum, given by Jane Bealby-Wright in 1950.

A Bacon family tree, from Joseph Bacon who settled in the Isle of Man in 1724 to the death of John Caesar Bacon in 1916, in bundle MDL 37/10 in the Manx Museum.

Collection of notes and letters assembled by Kenneth Whitehead in connection with his 1953 visit to the Isle of Man which led to his 1954 article in *Country Life.*

Collection of notes and letters assembled by Jack Quine from 1966 to 1988 in connection with his management of the museum flock.

Extracts from the Calf of Man Bird Observatory Annual Reports.

The will of Caesar Bacon, who died on 16th May 1916.

The will of Sir. Mark Collet, who died on 24th September 1944.

The will of Ellen Mary Marsh Gordon Cubbin, who died 21 May 1955.

A typed copy of a 3-page letter from Edward Christian of Northop to Sir Mark Collet (MS 1600 B, Manx Museum).

The entry for Sir Mark Collet in *Who was who ? 1941-1950.*

The entry for Sir John William Buchanan Jardine in *Who was who ? 1961-1970.*

Typescript copy of J.F. Robinson's report of his study of the Collet flock on Peel Hill, 1949.

The *Times* obituary to Sir Mark Collet, 27 September 1944.

Kent Messenger obituary to Sir Mark Collet.

The *Manx Examiner* obituary to Sir Mark Collet, 29 September 1944.

Introduction to the Collet family papers in the Kent Archives Office (U1287).

The *Annandale Herald and Record* obituary to Sir John Buchanan-Jardine, 5th November 1969.

Copies of record cards of Loghtans kept at Whipsnade Zoo provided by the Zoological Society of London.

RBST computer print-out of numbers of Manx Loghtans registered per year.

Letters in the Castlemilk estate letter books: 24 Oct, 29 Oct 1928; 12 March, 1 April, 23 July 1930; 18 Dec, 21 Dec 1933; 31 Aug 1934; 8 Oct 1936; 21 Sept, 7 Oct, 20 Oct, 31 Oct, 4 Nov, 10 Nov, 21 Nov 1955.

Notes

(1) Copies of all records and information assembled during the preparation of this book will be deposited in the library of the Manx Museum.

(2) In some respects details in this book differ from those in the article published in *The Ark* in March 1988; where there are discrepancies, recent research has modified these earlier conclusions.

Index

About the Author

Dr. Peter Wade-Martins has been breeding Manx Loghtans at his smallholding at North Elmham in Norfolk for ten years. While he is enthusiastic about the conservation of rare breeds, he feels it is also important to demonstrate their commercial potential wherever possible. He has about 25 Loghtans which run with about 70 or so pedigree Lleyns, a breed which was also rare before it enjoyed a commercial revival. For most seasons he has bred the Loghtans pure, but as supply overtook demand in the 1980s he experimented with cross breeding using a Suffolk ram. He has been most impressed with the results: 'you can stock the ewes quite heavily because the Manx is a small sheep, and then produce Suffolk cross lambs which show no sign of having come from a small primitive horned brown ewe'. This is where he feels the commercial future of the breed lies. 'They should not be treated just a pretty park sheep', he says. He joined the Rare Breeds Survival Trust as a member in 1978 and became a Sheep Flock Inspector for the *Combined Flock Book* in 1986. In 1988 he was elected as the first chairman of the newly-formed Manx Loghtan Sheep Breeders Group of the Trust.

Other spare time interests include vegetable gardening, welding and Ferguson tractors, for which he confesses a particular weakness. He is currently chairman of the local parish council. He also acts as archaeological consultant to the East Anglian office of the National Trust.

In his other life, as a professional archaeologist, he is an Assistant Director of the Norfolk Museums Service and County Field Archaeologist in charge of the Norfolk Archaeological Unit which runs rescue excavations and archaeological surveys in the county. 'We are becoming more involved in the conservation and interpretation of the historic landscape, rather than just excavating the bits which are about to be destroyed'. The publication of *Norfolk from the Air* (1987) edited by him was an attempt to explain the historic landscape to the people of Norfolk, and 'the public demand for the book has been extremely encouraging'. His own particular research interest is Anglo-Saxon and medieval settlements and settlement patterns, the subject of his Ph.D. thesis. He is a past chairman of the Standing Conference of Archaeological Unit Managers.

His wife, Dr. Susanna Wade Martins, has made a special study of the history of Norfolk agriculture and her first book was on the nineteenth-century management of the Holkham estate, *A Great Estate at Work* (1980). She followed this with *A History of Norfolk* (1984) and *Norfolk A Changing Countryside 1780-1914* (1988) and is currently completing a survey of Norfolk farm buildings and a biography of Turnip Townsend.

They have two sons of school age, Richard and Edward, who enjoy shepherding work. Family holidays on the Isle of Eigg in the Inner Hebrides inevitably led to a book of the history of the island called *Eigg: and island landscape* (1987), which has earned a Carnegie Interpret Britain award.